THE ELEVENTH COMMANDMENT

*A fresh look
at loving
your neighbor
as yourself*

DWIGHT K. NELSON

Pacific Press® Publishing Association
Nampa, Idaho
Oshawa, Ontario, Canada

Edited by B. Russell Holt
Designed by Dennis Ferree

ISBN 0-8163-1850-6

01 02 03 04 05 • 5 4 3 2 1

DEDICATION

To Skip

For being there . . . and here . . . all these years.

CONTENTS

A WORD BEFORE

My friend, Joe Engelkemier, in his wonderful book on prayer, *More and Still More: A Passion for All God Offers,* tells of a college coed who wrote the following letter home to her parents:

Dear Mom and Dad:

I'm sorry to be so long in writing. Unfortunately, all my stationery was destroyed the night our dorm was set on fire by the demonstrators. I'm out of the hospital now and the doctors say my eyesight should return—sooner or later. The wonderful boy, Bill, who rescued me from the fire, kindly offered to share his little apartment with me until the dorm is rebuilt. He comes from a good family, so you won't be surprised when I tell you we're going to be married. In fact, since you've always wanted a grandchild, you'll be glad to know that you'll be grandparents next month.

P.S. Please disregard the above practice in English composition. There was no fire; I haven't been in the hospital; I'm not pregnant; and I don't even have a steady boyfriend. But I did get a D in French and an F in Chemistry, and I just wanted to be sure you received this news in the proper perspective.

Perspective is everything, isn't it? That girl may have gotten a D in French and an F in chemistry, but she wins an A+ in logic and persuasion! I suggest she go into law—not chemical law or French law, you understand—just plain law will do. Because perspective makes all the difference in the world.

Which makes me wonder: Have we lost our perspective? Here we all are a part of a world tentatively, gingerly perhaps, taking its first small steps into a brand new millennium. They say the old is gone, the new has come. But has it really? After all these years, could it be that we've lost our perspective? Not the world now—I'm thinking of you and me.

I came across two dusty lines a summer ago. And I've been ruminating on them ever since. Two single lines spoken on the eve of a brutal death. But I wonder if the implications of these two lines aren't almost as brutal for what has been our traditional perspective as a community of faith!

And so for the next few pages please accept this invitation to journey with me past the threshhold of a new millennium. Let me be more direct—come brood with me. Let's muse over them together. Just two lines.

Because I am deeply convicted that these two lines proffer both the potential and the power to permanently change our perspective. So radical are they, in fact, that they may end up changing not only *how* but also *where* we will spend the next millennium!

Dwight K. Nelson
Berrien Springs, Michigan
New Year's Day, A.D. 2001

I *give you*
a new commandment,
that you love one another.
Just as I have loved you,
you also should love
one another.' "

JOHN 13:34

THE ELEVENTH COMMANDMENT

I made my way to the back of our commuter flight from South Bend, Indiana to Chicago. The ticket stub indicated I had been assigned (consigned to, really) the last row. A middle-aged gentleman in a suit and tie was already occupying the aisle seat, so I crawled over him to the window. As I did so, I noticed that he had stuck his ticket stub up into the frame of his glasses, no doubt as an act of public protest over his own consignment to the back of the plane.

Looking for an excuse to visit with him, I tapped him on the shoulder and asked if we were all supposed to affix our stubs in our glasses as he was modeling. He laughed. And we fell into conversation. He was a management consultant for Fortune 500 companies. And I was on my way to a speaking engagement across the country. He was a Jew; I a Christian.

"And what will you be speaking on?" he queried.

"The eleventh commandment," I responded.

"The eleventh commandment?" he exclaimed incredulously. "Good grief! We have a hard enough time with the Ten. What would we ever do with an eleventh!"

A very good question this Jewish gentleman raises. I wonder, "What *would* we do with the eleventh commandment?"

A new commandment

Another Jew, and truly another gentleman (though this One much younger), is about to speak. He will be dead in less than twenty-four hours—and He knows it. And when a man knows he's about to die, you can be sure his final words will be fraught and heavy with that which he feels most deeply about. Because when you're counting down to death, every word counts.

So for Jesus tonight, here in the torch-lit upper room, what matters most of all is on His heart last of all: " 'I give you a new commandment, that you love one another. Just as I have loved you, you also should love one another. By this everyone will know that you are my disciples, if you have love for one another.' "[1]

What is on the heart of the Man who will soon be dead? "I give you a new commandment, that you love one another."

In case you might be tempted to conclude this command to love is simply an aside, just a passing and isolated thought by the Master, you need to know that here within these four upper-room walls Jesus will issue this command five times—Love one another . . . love one another . . . love one another . . . love one another . . . love one another.[2]

And when you read the context for those five Crucifixion-eve commands from Jesus, you can't help notice how often the word "love" appears in those upper-room chapters. So much so that I decided to count them, circling every time the word "love" or one of its derivatives appeared in Jesus' words and prayer in John

13 through 17. In my translation I counted "love" thirty-three times, thirty-one of which were on His death-row lips. It is inescapable: Love is clearly, unequivocally on the Master's mind on the eve of the Master's death. "I give you a new commandment, that you love one another."

But I know what you're thinking—"Come on, what's the big deal here? I mean, ho hum and whoopee! We've all heard this one before. 'Love one another.' This is hardly a grand new revelation we've never thought of. Why, it's as traditional and obvious as motherhood and apple pie!"

And of course, you're absolutely right. When this upper-room command finally got my attention, I realized that this is no new command at all. We've known it for years. And in fact, so had the disciples. After all, millennia earlier God Himself had thundered from Sinai's rocky crag the command, "Thou shalt love thy neighbor as thyself."[3] And Jesus Himself had reiterated those same ancient words in His own teaching and preaching earlier in His life.[4]

Radical love

But what will make this old command so dramatically "new" for these upper-room disciples is that in less than twenty-four hours they will be witnesses to a bloody love so radical that it will forever rewrite the definition of "love" in the human language.

President Ronald Reagan, that grand communicator of the Oval Office some years ago, touched the heart of the nation when he quoted the upper-room words of Jesus. Remember that tragic Air Florida crash one winter into the icy Potomac River just off the runway of National Airport in Washington, D.C.? Rescue helicopters and news cameras hovered over the frigid, wind-swept waters of the Potomac, as survivors of the crash fought to the surface amidst ice and debris.

A lifeline was lowered to one of the bobbing, surviving passengers, a bald-headed man. But instead of grasping that line to safety, he tossed the attached lifering across the waves and ice to another struggling victim nearby. The rescue helicopter dragged that fortunate survivor to safety. Back came the lifeline, and again it was dropped to the same bald-headed man. And again, he passed the ring to yet another desperate victim. Again, another survivor was rescued.

Back and forth that drama of life and death played. But when the helicopter returned one last time to rescue the unselfish stranger, he was gone. The frigid death waters had finally claimed him.

Intoning that stranger's unselfish bravery, President Reagan in a national address quoted Jesus, "Greater love hath no man than this, that a man lay down his life for his friends."[5]

Those were the crimson words of Christ spoken in that same upper room just moments after He had declared His " 'new commandment, that you love one another.' "[6] An old commandment that would become forever new on the morrow, when those eleven men would witness no "greater love" than the brutal glory of the Man on the middle cross who "lay down his life for his friends."

Calvary has forever rewritten the definition of "love" in the human language.

The ultimate defining characteristic

But may I be candid with you? For me, the newness of Jesus' command to love one another isn't found so much in His radical redefinition of love—both human and divine—on the cross the next day, as utterly glorious as His sacrificial love was and still is and will ever be. But as I brood on His upper-room words, what is so painfully new to me is the realization of what Jesus is actually declaring to be *the ultimate defining and identifying characteristic* of His true followers on earth.

" 'By this everyone will know that you are my disciples, if you have love for one another.' "7

What is so new and painful is woefully evident when you realize what Jesus does *not* say!

Please note that Jesus does *not* say, "By this the whole world will know that you are My people—*if you keep the seventh-day Sabbath.*" He certainly could have said it. For I remind you that He is talking tonight to a thoroughly sabbatarian group of followers. All eleven disciples have kept the seventh-day Sabbath from their very first breath. And all eleven disciples will keep the seventh-day Sabbath until their very last breath. But strangely Jesus does not declare, "By this the whole world will know that you are My people—*if you keep the seventh-day Sabbath.*" Of course He's Lord of the Sabbath. Of course He will rest in the tomb on the very day He, as Creator, gave to the human race long ages before. But note it carefully and prayerfully, fellow sabbatarians, Christ did not make the seventh-day Sabbath the ultimate defining characteristic of His true followers.

When a man is on death row, he chooses his words very carefully. And the words Jesus intentionally chose were these: "By this everyone will know that you are my disciples, if you have love for one another."

Just as strangely Jesus does *not* declare, "By this the whole world will know that you are My people—*if your hope is in my second coming.*" Of course that's the great and blessed hope that has flamed brightly in the hearts of Christ's disciples throughout the millennia. Why, just moments later in that same upper room Jesus will declare the beloved promise, " 'Let not your heart be troubled; you believe in God, believe also in Me. In my Father's house are many mansions . . . I go to prepare a place for you. And if I go and prepare a place for you, I will come again and receive you to Myself; that where I am, there you may be also.' "[8]

Mark it well: Jesus neither denigrates nor denies either the seventh-day Sabbath or the blessed Advent hope here in the upper room. *But He will not make either of those grand and glorious truths the ultimate identifying mark of His people on earth.* You may call yourself a Seventh-day Adventist, as I do, but neither the "Seventh-day" nor the "Adventist" is how Jesus declared the world will recognize you. Or me.

"By this everyone will know that you are my disciples, if you have love for one another."

Please note that Jesus does *not* declare on that fateful Thursday night in the upper room, "By this the whole world will know that you are My people—*if you believe and teach the cleansing of the sanctuary and the final judgment before I return to earth.*" I remind you that every single one of the eleven disciples listening to Him that night is a firm believer in Yom Kippur and the Day of Atonement's motif of cleansing and judgment. They know the sanctuary service inside out. But strangely, the Master does not commend their sanctuary truth as the defining mark of how the world will identify His people.

"By this everyone will know that you are my disciples, if you have love for one another."

The truth that is so painfully obvious in Jesus' final injunction and command to His disciples is made all the more compelling by noting what Jesus does *not* declare: "By this the whole world will know that you are My people—*if you embrace the twenty-seven fundamental beliefs.*" Christ could have listed any of them or all of them as the identifying mark of His people on earth. For all twenty-seven great truths are just as true today as they were that night long ago.

But He does not. Instead we read His unmistakable, unequivocal, unconditional declaration that night: "By this all—red and yellow, black and white—by this all—rich and poor, educated and illiterate—by this all—first world, second world, third world—by this all the world will know you are My people—if you have love for one another."

A loving people?

So, the question begs to be asked: Are we a loving people?

Or are we, as Mark Twain cynically put it, "good in the worst sense of the word"? You've known people like that, haven't you (present company excepted, of course!)? People who are so right in their truth. So correct in their orthodoxy. So proper in their observances and standards. But my oh my, who would ever want to live next door to them! Those people who are "good in the worst sense of the word."

Like the little English girl prayed: "O God, make the bad people good . . . and the good people nice."

"By this all the world will know that you are My people, if you have love for one another."

Are we a nice people?

Are we a loving people?

Or are we "good in the worst sense of the word"?

Philip Yancey, in his stirring book, *What's So Amazing About Grace?*, tells a true story he heard from a friend who works with the down-and-out in Chicago:

A prostitute came to me in wretched straits, homeless, sick, unable to buy food for her two-year-old daughter. Through sobs and tears, she told me she had been renting out her daughter–two years old!–to men interested in kinky sex. She made more renting out her daughter for an hour than she could earn on her own in a night. She had to do it, she said, to support her own drug habit. I could hardly bear hearing her sordid story. For one thing, it made me legally liable—I'm required to report cases of child abuse. I had no idea what to say to this woman.

At last I asked if she had ever thought of going to a church for help. I will never forget the look of pure, naïve shock that crossed her face. "Church!" she cried. "Why would I ever go there? I was already feeling terrible about myself. They'd just make me feel worse."

Yancey then reflects:

What struck me about my friend's story is that women much like this prostitute flew toward Jesus, not away from him. The worse a person felt about herself, the more likely she saw Jesus as a refuge. Has the church lost that gift? Evidently the down-and-out, who flocked to Jesus when he lived on earth, no longer feel welcome among his followers. What has happened?[9]

And what shall we say in response? Some may be tempted to suggest that the problem was really with those churches that the poor hapless mother had come to know. Why, if she had known *our* church, she'd have thought differently! Oh, really?

May I share a letter with you? I received it from a woman I met at an out-of-town preaching engagement not too long ago.

Dear Pastor Nelson,
About five years ago, another close friend of mine died of AIDS. His name was Jack, and he died at the age of

thirty-four. Jack was baptized as an Adventist about fifteen months before he died, and I knew him mainly from the weekly prayer meetings. Jack was infected with HIV several years prior to his joining the church. . . . He never knew he had HIV until he got pneumonia. He survived the pneumonia, met some neighbors of his who were Adventists, and came into the truth through them.

Unfortunately, a few members of the church couldn't accept Jack because he had AIDS. Some stopped going to church and prayer meetings because he was there, and they feared catching AIDS from the air or sitting in the same room as him. My former pastor . . . tried very hard to educate these people—but they didn't want to hear it. When Pastor . . . spent time in the hospital with Jack every day before he passed away, they would say something like: "I hope our Pastor won't get AIDS in the hospital and then come back and give it to all of us!" How angels must weep in heaven for the hardness of hearts, even of professed Christians!

Thank the Lord, Jack remained faithful until the end and even had a spirit of love and forgiveness toward those members who shunned him. Jack knew how much Jesus loved him, and that was enough.

" 'I give you a new commandment, that you love one another. Just as I have loved you, you also should love one another. By this everyone will know that you are my disciples, if you have love for one another.' "[10]

I realize that the story of the desperate mother and the story of the dying young man could be aberrations or exceptions to the general rule of life where you and I "live and move and have our being." And I'd quickly write them both off as such were it not for the troubling awareness that all too often I have not loved—publicly or privately—as Jesus would have done were He in my place. I have been far too quick to judge someone else and only too eager to whisper my criticisms to another listening ear. I have condemned those with whom I've disagreed, and belittled those whose tastes are not my own. I have hurried by those who have waited for a word of compassion, of caring, even just a smile of love—hurrying about my Father's business without my Father's heart. I have pretended to be tolerant of all races and cultures, all the while dismissing as lesser gods those who are different from me.

Sure, I'd love to dismiss both stories as flukes were it not for my own heart—that I know all too well.

How did the letter writer end her story of Jack? "Jack knew how much Jesus loved him, and that was enough."

But in the end is it *really* enough? "By this everyone will know that you are my disciples, if you have love for one another." Apparently for Jesus it *isn't* enough that the world knows His love. Apparently for Him it is enough only when they know our love too.

A change in perspective

And so at this dawning of a new millennium, isn't it time we change our perspective?

Let me ask you an embarrassing question: In our exuberance to help the world remember the fourth commandment, have we forgotten to remember the eleventh? While we champion obedience to the Ten Commandments, do we all the while disobey the eleventh commandment?

"I give you a new commandment, that you love one another." The eleventh commandment. It takes neither a theologian nor a sociologist to observe that humanity today simply isn't clamoring for the Ten Commandments. But human beings the world over are starving for the eleventh commandment. If God would win their minds, we must first win their hearts.

For as that classic on the life of Jesus, *The Desire of Ages,* puts it:

> Love to man is the earthward manifestation of the love of God. It was to impart this love, to make us children of one family, that the King of glory became one with us. And when His parting words are fulfilled, 'Love one another, as I have loved you' (John 15:12); when we love the world as He has loved it, then for us His mission is accomplished. We are fitted for heaven; for we have heaven in our hearts.[11]

"By this the world will know that you are My people, if you have love for one another."

The telephone rang in our office at Pioneer Memorial Church. My secretary buzzed me on the intercom—the call was for me, though she didn't recognize the woman's voice or name. Neither did I as I listened to this stranger begin with the familiar words, "I need some help."

I steeled myself (I'm sorry to confess), waiting for the other shoe about money to drop. And it did. She was a mother of two teenagers. And she had been listening to our live services on the radio on Saturday mornings. She'd heard the sermons about God not being Someone to be afraid of, but Someone to be a friend of. And she wondered if people who believed in a God like that could help her. (I swallowed hard.) She needed money. (I knew it!)

Although—she went on—she actually had a thousand dollars waiting for her in Chicago. But after hearing about God on our broadcast, she felt it would no longer be right for her to retrieve the thousand dollars owed her.

It turns out the woman, in desperation, had resorted to the only profession she could think of to keep food on her table. And in the shadowy doorways of the Windy City she had been plying her wares as a prostitute. But now she wanted to change. She needed help.

To this day I thank God He gave me the presence of mind not to hang up with a quick referral as soon as I realized she wanted money. Instead I listened to her story. And when she was through, I assured her we would help, making arrangements for her to receive some emergency funds. And then I forgot all about it and her.

Until weeks later, when a woman came up to me after our services and introduced herself. I didn't recognize her, until she replayed the telephone conversation. Of course I remembered! With a smile she announced that she and her children had begun worshiping with our congregation.

Nobody knew her story. Weeks and months went by. Nobody knew even on that sunlit Sabbath when she rose out of the waters of our baptistry, "a new creation" in Christ—"everything old [had] passed away; see, everything [had] become new."[12]

Today she heads up one of our congregation's outreach care ministries. And whenever I see her, I am grateful to God that for at least one day He kept me from breaking the eleventh commandment.

Lewis Smedes has written: "God weeps when people think they can love *only* him. He is the first to admit that he alone is not enough for man or woman. People need people as surely as they need God. Because God knows this, his redemptive love creates a company of love-sharers."[13]

I love that. In a world starving for love God has raised up "a company of love-sharers." Which is precisely why Jesus gave His eleventh commandment to His church in the beginning. And to His church in the end.

" 'I give you a new commandment, that you love one another. Just as I have loved you, you also should love one another. By this everyone will know that you are my disciples, if you have love for one another.' "[14]

Because in the end, there is no other way the world will know the truth about Jesus. Or His church.

———

1. John 13:34, 35. Unless otherwise indicated, all scriptural references are from the *New Revised Standard Version.*

2. John 13:34, 35; 15:12, 17.

3. Leviticus 19:18, KJV.

4. Matthew 22:39; Mark 12:31.

5. John 15:13, KJV.

6. John 13:34.

7. John 13:35.

8. See John 14:1-3, NKJ.

9. Philip Yancey, *What's So Amazing About Grace?* p. 11.

10. John 13:34, 35.

11. Ellen White, *The Desire of Ages,* p. 641.

12. 2 Corinthians 5:17.

13. Lewis Smedes, *Love Within Limits,* p. 26, emphasis his.

14. John 13:34, 35.

I *give you*

a new commandment,

that you love one another.

Just as I have loved you,

you also should love

one another.' "

JOHN 13:34

CHAPTER

2

TEN DOZEN TOES
AT THE
SECRET SHRINE

A few months ago I received an anonymous letter. Normally I wouldn't even read it, let alone share it, since I was taught early on that letters like this, with no signature, are best filed in the circular file. After all, why give attention to an idea that not even the author is willing to own up to!

Well, I'm glad I didn't throw *this* letter away. Because I have read and reread it and read it again. Why? See for yourself:

> Dear Dwight:
>
> As I listened to you preach last Sabbath, I couldn't help but wonder who the "Christ" of Dwight Nelson is? This little book [the anonymous writer attached a photocopied booklet] . . . reminds of a truth that is little known and often resisted in our day, that following Jesus is about becoming nothing. As the book states: "There is no way for Christ to live in me, and be ev-

erything, unless I am willing for self to be nothing."

God has used you, Dwight, through Net98. . . . [But] God wants to do more *through* you instead of *by* you, if you will let Him. Considering the limelight you have enjoyed, I can imagine your difficulty in further embracing nothingness, and the challenge of calling your church family to join you in that pursuit. . . .

As I look around the university and what looks too often like superficial godliness, ongoing differences and divisions, a grasping after things, and having "my way," one cannot help but feel that self is too alive.

I don't think your parishioners will welcome the call for self dying—none of us do—but it is a message desperately needed.

I pray you will ask God where you stand in all of this. . . .

I wish you the best,
A Fellow Traveler

Now can you see why I didn't throw the letter away? Because the writer is right. How can I argue with him or with her? But what shall I do with this anonymous appeal? What shall *we* do with it?

Living the eleventh commandment

The answer lies in a dramatically un-anonymous moment there in the torch-lit upper room. It surely will go down in history as one of the most graphic and effective "show and tell" exhibits of all time! Not surprisingly, though, we hardly ever recall it whenever we read the eleventh commandment. After all, the crescendo of the last evening and the Last Supper keeps building forward, not backward.

And yet, when it comes to *living* the eleventh commandment, it is only in going backward that we will ever learn how to move forward. The secret to the anonymous letter is to go backward.

" 'I give you a new commandment, that you love one another. Just as I have loved you, you also should love one another. By this everyone will know that you are my disciples, if you have love for one another.' "[1]

Did you catch Jesus' backward glance? Because you and I live post-Calvary, we tend to read the Cross into every reference to divine love. And that is only natural. But we make a mistake doing that with the eleventh commandment. Because tonight Jesus speaks plainly and clearly to His disciples: I want you to love each other "just as I *have* loved you." (The Greek can actually be translated, "just as I *loved* you." In the past. Period.)

So what was it in the past that would be on every one of their minds that night?

Greatness through humility

Of that evening the record reads: "And when the hour came, [Jesus] took his place at the table, and the apostles with him. . . . A dispute also arose among them as to which one of them was to be regarded as the greatest."[2] In less than twenty-four hours, Jesus will die a cruel and savage death. This is His last night on earth with His dearest friends. But they still don't get it! And I blush when I have to admit that neither do we. Do we?

"But he said to them, 'The kings of the Gentiles lord it over them; and those in authority over them are called benefactors. But not so with you; rather the greatest among you must become like the youngest, and the leader like one who serves.' "[3]

In the Jewish home, the youngest serves the older siblings,

which is also true in most American homes—unless, of course, the youngest is a girl, as my brother and I learned soon enough. But normally, everyone knows the youngest is the designated resident "Gofor"—go for this, go for that, etc. Jesus' point is unsubtle: If you want to be great, then *you* be the "gofor"!

" 'For who is greater, the one who is at the table or the one who serves? Is it not the one at the table? But I am among you as one who serves.' "[4]

And then to prove what He had just said, there comes the high and electric drama of John 13. Commentators are clear that Luke 22 and John 13 are parallel accounts of the same moment in that upper room.

"[Jesus] got up from the table, took off his outer robe, and tied a towel around himself. Then he poured water into a basin and began to wash the disciples' feet and to wipe them with the towel that was tied around him."[5]

You know the story, don't you? The servant, who was supposed to be on hand to perform this most menial of tasks, didn't show! The task of washing the feet was so menial, by the way, that if you were a Jewish master with both Jewish and Gentile slaves or servants, it was commonly understood that your Jewish servants were exempted from having to wash your feet, leaving the Gentile slaves to perform that task. On occasion wives and children would wash the husband and father's feet, but never the other way around.

Which is what makes this moment so stunning! A Jewish master, who clearly is revered as Master by His own disciples, has stripped to the waist and is now bowing down at the feet of His Jewish disciples and is performing the servile task clearly relegated by social mores to bottom-rung Gentile slaves!

Which is precisely why Peter refuses to let Jesus continue!

He came to Simon Peter, who said to him, "Lord, are you [emphatic in the Greek] going to wash my feet?" Jesus answered, "You do not know now what I [emphatic in the Greek] am doing, but later you will understand." Peter said to him, "You will never [a double negative in the Greek to capture Peter's loud protest—you will *no not!*] wash my feet." Jesus answered, "Unless I wash you, you have no share with me." Simon Peter [true to his boisterous speak-now-think-later form] said to him, "Lord, not my feet only but also my hands and my head [Gimme a bath]!" Jesus said to him, "One who has bathed does not need to wash, except for the feet, but is entirely clean. And you are clean, though not all of you." For he knew who was to betray him; for this reason he said, "Not all of you are clean."

After he had washed their feet, and put on his robe, and had returned to the table, he said to them, "Do you know what I have done to you?"[6]

Makes you wonder, doesn't it? Do *we* know what Jesus just did?

Loving as Jesus loves

I don't want to sound irreverent, but what would happen if we attempted to psychoanalyze Jesus for a moment? Not that we would be all that effective at it. But for a moment what if we attempted to get into Jesus' mind, to probe His psyche, to find out the thought patterns of His inner life? After all, didn't He command us to love one another just as He loved us? But how can we know how to love others until we understand how He truly loved us?

Fortunately for us, the Gospel of John exposes the inner life and mind of Jesus as no other Gospel does. And though the words "humble" and "humility" are never used by John, clearly what emerges in his Gospel is a profound definition of that upper-room humility that Jesus declares is how we are to love one another.

Examine the following statements of Jesus in the Gospel of John and notice the intentional way in which He keeps referring to His relationship with the Father. Carefully note how often Jesus uses the words "not" and "nothing" in connection with Himself:

> John 5:19—"Very truly, I tell you, the Son can do *nothing* on his own."
> John 5:30—"I can do *nothing* on my own. . . . I seek to do *not* my own will."
> John 5:41—"I do *not* accept glory from human beings."
> John 6:38—"I have come down from heaven, *not* to do my own will."
> John 7:16—"My teaching is *not* mine."
> John 7:28—"I have *not* come on my own."
> John 8:28—"I do *nothing* on my own."
> John 8:42—"I did *not* come on my own, but he sent me."
> John 8:50—"I do *not* seek my own glory."
> John 14:10—"The words that I say to you I do *not* speak on my own."
> John 14:24—"The word that you hear is *not* mine."

Count them—twelve times Jesus publicly negates Himself in honor of the Father. Andrew Murray, the South African divine of the last century who noted these twelve intentional negations of Jesus in his stirring book, *Humility,* draws this conclusion:

> Christ was nothing, that God might be all. He resigned Himself with His will and His powers entirely for the Father to work in Him. Of His own power, His own will, and His own glory, of His whole mission with all His works and His teaching, He said, "It is not I; I am nothing; I have given Myself to the Father to work. I am nothing, the Father is all."[7]

So when Jesus stoops to wash the ten dozen toes of His subordinates, when the Master bows down at the soiled feet of His disciples and dirties Himself in order to serve them, what we are witnessing is the intentional self-abandonment of Jesus. He who made Himself nothing before His Father in heaven humbles Himself and becomes as nothing before His own followers. Radical humility—how else shall we describe such abasement by the incarnate God! He willingly makes Himself *nothing* so that those He loves—whether God or man—might become *everything.*

Over and over in the Gospel of John, Jesus reiterates His nothingness. And then to prove it, He washes our feet! So foreign is this radical concept, this stunning portrait, to our selfish hearts that Jesus has to ask us, " 'Do you know what I have done to you?' "[8]

Do we? Do we know the meaning of this kind of radical humility born of self-abandoning love?

The shrine of self

Attached to the anonymous letter was a sheath of quotations, including this disturbing one from L. E. Maxwell:

The church world is full of Christian professors and ministers, Sunday school teachers and workers, evangelists and missionaries, in whom the gifts of the Spirit are very manifest, and who bring blessing to multitudes, but who, when known "up close," are found to be full of self. They may have "forsaken all" for Christ and imagine they would be ready, like the disciples of old, to die for their Master; but deep down in their hidden, private lives there lurks that dark sinister power of self. . . . Such persons may wonder, all the while why they do not have victory over their wounded pride, their touchiness, their greediness, their lovelessness, their failure to experience the promised "rivers of living water." Ah, the secret is not far away. They secretly and habitually practice "shrine worship"—at the shrine of self. There they bow daily and do obeisance. They are fundamental. In the outward Cross they glory, but inwardly they worship another god—stretch out their hands to serve a pitied, petted, and pampered self-life.[9]

Having grown up in Japan for fourteen years and having lived another three years on the island of Singapore, I have visited many shrines. You know what a shrine is, don't you? It's a miniature temple that usually houses a local god or a community idol, a "holy" place along the way where travelers and worshipers may pause to genuflect or say prayers or burn incense, day or night.

Which is why L. E. Maxwell's metaphor is so embarrassing and painful! He suggests we Christians are no different than the Oriental—for we, too, have our own private secret shrines where we can secretly genuflect in front of our own mirrored images. Where we can privately idolize and worship self. Where, hidden from public view, we can burn incense and stretch out our hands to self all day long. Where we can be, as he put it, a "church full of Christian professors and ministers and workers who serve a pitied, petted, and pampered self-life."

Do we worship at the secret shrine of "a pitied, petted, and pampered self-life"? Is that the prevailing sin of our churches, our marriages, our lives? Too much of self, far too much of self—is that it?

J. Gregory Mantle in his book, *Beyond Humiliation,* makes this most provocative observation:

> Many in their eagerness to succeed, are continually crying to God for the gift of spiritual power. But God cannot fulfill their desire, for He is a jealous God, and will not give His glory to another; and [what is more] to trust men and women with spiritual power who are full of self assertion would only be to feed their vanity and promote their self-idolization and love of self-display.[10]

If God granted this church the power we languish for and the prestige we long for, our secret shrines would become a sprawling temple for our own self-worship. We have a hard enough time as it is incessantly calling in the media on our cell phones and faxing out our glowing press releases—"Come and see what *we* have done."

But as God cries out through Isaiah, "I am the LORD, that is my name; my glory I give to no other, nor my praise to idols."[11] Think of what He could have done, or might yet do, were the church not so cluttered and clogged with the vanity of our secret shrines! "My glory I give to no other." No wonder He cannot yet trust us with unmitigated success.

"After he had washed their feet, and put on his robe, and had returned to the table, he said to them, 'Do you know what I have done to you?' "[12] Do we? Do we know the meaning of such self-emptying humility and love? And how in the end can this radical humility of Christ teach me how to love as the eleventh commandment commands me to?

I have pondered that question for some time now, and as a result of that reflection let me share with you four specific actions you and I can take in our quest to become humble like Jesus—to live like the Master, that we might love like the Master.

Action #1—Ask for humility and help

I found a touching prayer for you to copy and keep in your Bible, as I now do in mine. It's in the inspirational book, *Christ's Object Lessons*:

No outward observances can take the place of simple faith and entire renunciation of self. But no man can empty himself of self. We can only consent for Christ to accomplish the work. Then the language of the soul will be, *Save me in spite of myself, my weak, unchristlike self. Lord, take my heart; for I cannot give it. It is Thy property. Keep it pure, for I cannot keep it for Thee. Mold me, fashion me, raise me into a pure and holy atmosphere, where the rich current of Thy love can flow through my soul.*[13]

Isn't that a beautiful prayer? Self cannot cast out self. Like every alcoholic, we need a "higher power." "Save me in spite of myself, my weak, unchristlike self." What a prayer to repeat every new morning. Action #1 is *ask* for humility and help.

Action #2—Embrace all that humbles you

I learned this one from Andrew Murray. Several years ago one of our students gave me his book *Humility*. As I have read and reread it three times, I've found it to be an encouraging and empowering volume for anyone who longs to become like the humble Jesus. Murray writes:

> Place yourself before God in your utter helplessness. Consent heartily to the fact of your weakness to slay or make yourself alive. Sink down into your own nothingness, in the spirit of meek and patient and trustful surrender to God. Accept every humiliation, look upon every fellow-man who tries or vexes you, as a means of grace to humble use. Use every opportunity of humbling yourself before your fellow-men as a help to remain humble before God.[14]

I can testify that when I have remembered Murray's point, I have found it really does work. Namely, when something goes wrong in my life, when I fail in a project, when I embarrass myself in front of others, when I am hurt, when I feel humiliated—Andrew Murray has taught me that if I will embrace whatever or whoever humiliates or humbles me, if I will thank God for that humiliation, the normal, carnal pride paradigm in my mind gets shifted. And when it does, the sting of that humiliation actually dissipates.

Because, what happens is you play the game, as it were, by a new set of rules. And now instead of going through life trying to *keep* your pride from getting wounded, you come to realize that the goal of the Christian journey is precisely the opposite—to *get* your pride wounded, or rather, crucified! "I have been crucified with Christ; and it is no longer I [*ego,* the first personal pronoun in the Greek] who live, but it is Christ who lives in me."[15] Look, it doesn't take a rocket scientist or a theologian to know that if your pride just got wounded, it's proof enough that there was enough pride there to get wounded in the first place!

So embrace what humbles you, what wounds your pride. Once we're able to thank God for our failures, we're no longer embarrassed to face them or to talk about them with others. We no longer have to maintain an "invincible" or "infallible" front. Pride no longer needs to prove itself, in order to be accepted by others. Instead, humility rejoices that we are now "accepted in the beloved."[16]

Then we can pray, "Thank You, God, for letting me get humbled, for that is truly what I want to become—humble like Jesus." Action #2 is *embrace* what humbles you.

Action #3—Seek to become low and weak and nothing

That is exactly what Jesus did when He took the initiative in the upper room and took on the role of a slave, becoming low and weak and nothing before the others.

Someone once asked that great prayer warrior and man of faith, George Muller, what was the secret of his life of service. To which Muller replied, " 'There was a day when I died;' and as he spoke, he bent lower, until he almost touched the floor. Continuing, he added, 'died to George Muller, his opinions, preferences, tastes and will; died to the world, its approval or censure; died to the approval or blame even of my brethren and friends; and since then I have studied only to show myself approved unto God.' "[17]

Seek to become low and weak and nothing. Jump at the opportunity to serve someone else. You be the one to stop and help the driver with the flat tire. You give up your place in that checkout line for that impatient soul farther back. You be the one to miss your plane because the stranger at the gate is obviously sick and needs someone to get her to help. Do yourself what in the past you have delegated purely as a sign of your authority over a subordinate. (I'm not suggesting that we quit delegating, but that we get our hands dirty washing the feet of those who report to us.)

Too often the reason I don't stop to help you, to listen to you, to love you really, is because I've been fooled into thinking that somehow I'm more important than you, that in some twisted economy I'm greater than you. "And if I stooped to wash his feet," or "if I stopped to take her place, what would all the others think?" That was the crippling worry that paralyzed an upper room full of hearts on the eve of a tragic death.

Until Someone stooped down and became a slave in order to set those enslaved hearts free. We can't love like Him until we live like Him. Action #3 is to *seek* to become low and weak and nothing.

Action #4—Reflect on the humility of Calvary

God is the most humble Being in the universe. Name for me one other person you can think of who is more humble than God. There is no one!

The cross of Jesus is proof that humility is the shining pinnacle of God's character! Yes, we celebrate His love. But we sinners would never have known His love had it not been for His humility in descending (con-descending) to this hellish outcropping in the universe we call home sweet home.

For that reason Paul sang out the truth: "Let the same mind be in you that was in Christ Jesus, who . . . emptied himself, taking the form of a slave. . . . And being found in human form, he humbled himself and became obedient to the point of death— even death on a cross."[18] The God of Calvary is the most humble Being you will ever meet!

As Roy Hession has written in his powerful little book, *The Calvary Road*:

> At the foot of the Cross is a low door, so low that to get through it one has to stoop and crawl through. It is the only entrance to the Highway. We must go through it, if we would go any further on our way. This door is called the Door of the Broken Ones. Only the broken can enter the Highway. To be broken means, "not I, but Christ."[19]

At every new day's dawning bow at the foot of the cross and reflect on the radical humility of Christ's radical love. Thanks to my late friend, Roger Morneau, I now read the Calvary story in Matthew 27:24-54 every single morning. Because it occurs to me that bowing before such self-emptying love is the first step toward loving others just as He has loved me.

" 'I give you a new commandment, that you love one another. Just as I have loved you, you also should love one another. By this everyone will know that you are my disciples, if you have love for one another.' "[20]

Morris Venden, the beloved and popular preacher of our generation, was on our Andrews University campus last fall to deliver the H.M.S. Richards lectureship on preaching. He recounted the time when as a young pastor he sat on the front row of a convocation where that great and aged Bible preacher and Voice of Prophecy radio speaker, H.M.S. Richards, Sr., was being interviewed. In the course of the interview, Dr. Richards was asked: "How would you sum up the message that the Seventh-day Adventist Church is to take to the world?"

Richards paused for but a second and then replied with two words: "Jesus only."

The same two words that sum up the truth about humility and love and the eleventh commandment. "Jesus only." And a generation of anonymous men and women and young adults and teenagers who have chosen to live for "Jesus only."

---

1. John 13:34, 35.
2. Luke 22:14, 24.
3. Luke 22:25, 26.
4. Luke 22:27.
5. John 13:4, 5.
6. John 13:6-12.
7. Andrew Murray, *Humility*, p. 23.
8. John 13:12.
9. L. E. Maxwell, *Born Crucified*, pp. 55, 56.
10. J. Gregory Mantle, *Beyond Humiliation*, pp. 111, 112.
11. Isaiah 42:8.
12. John 13:12.
13. Ellen White, *Christ's Object Lessons*, p. 159, emphasis supplied.
14. Andrew Murray, *Humility*, pp. 75, 76.
15. Galatians 2:19, 20.
16. Ephesians 1:6 KJV.
17. Quoted in Maxwell, p. 60.
18. Philippians 2:5-8.
19. Roy Hession, *Calvary Road*, p. 47.
20. John 13:34, 35.

I *give you
a new commandment,
that you love one another.
Just as I have loved you,
you also should love
one another.' "*

JOHN 13:34

CHAPTER 3

A TASTE OF NEW WINE

Edwina Humphrey Flynn, a classical vocalist, was our guest here at Andrews University last fall. A gifted musician, she came to us from her home in the heart of the Big Apple, New York City. She came to sing her heart out for the Master. And that she did movingly in an evening concert in the Pioneer Memorial Church. In the midst of her singing, she told a story. It is so dramatic and compelling a testimony of what can happen when a man or a woman chooses to live with a passion for Jesus Christ, that I must share it with you.

The light of His presence

It was Edwina's first day of school at the New York Conservatory. Early that morning at home she prayed that God would shine through her to all she would meet that opening day. Riding the crowded early-morning subway to downtown New York, she disembarked and hurried to the conservatory and her music classes.

THE ELEVENTH COMMANDMENT

Several weeks later on a day off, Edwina decided to go back downtown to the school and practice her vocal routines in one of the conservatory practice rooms. With the students away, she could practice alone and uninterrupted. Soon her melodious voice was ranging up and down her warm-up scales.

Suddenly it seemed as if she could hear distant voices. Strange. No one was supposed to be in the building that day. But sure enough, there were voices. She could hear them now. Voices that seemed to be drawing nearer down the empty hallway. Angry voices. She held her breath. The sounds of a heated argument grew louder and louder. Until finally it seemed as if the fury was now standing on the other side of the door from her.

Then, with a bang, her practice room door flew open and they burst in—four of them, as it turned out, fellow music students at the conservatory. "Ah, I knew you were here!" a young man triumphantly announced. And without an apology, he plunged on, "You see, we're having an argument over which is more powerful for good—black magic or white magic!" They were a group of young witches and warlocks (male witches), and had been debating the "values" of the occult.

Edwina, recovering from the shock of their surprise entry, was nonplused. "But what's that have to do with me? I know nothing about black or white magic!"

"Oh, but I know you're somebody special," the young spokesman for the group retorted. "Because I remember seeing you on the first day of classes. I happened to be in the station when you got off the subway that morning. And when I saw you, there was a glowing light that surrounded you and seemed to go ahead of you."

Incredulous, Edwina countered, "But how did you know I was here in the building today?"

"We were outside the conservatory a few minutes ago, arguing, when I noticed an unusual light shining out from under the conservatory door. I recognized it as the same light that surrounded you the day you got off the subway. I knew you had to be inside."

Can you believe it! The humble testimony of a friend of Jesus, who discovered—quite unbeknown to her—that the light of His presence in her life had actually been seen! What she had prayed for that first morning had been supernaturally answered.

Here's a no-brainer of a question: Wouldn't you like to experience such a closeness with Jesus that His life and His light and His love would actually radiate from your life, too?

I would, too!

No other identifying mark

How can we experience that kind of closeness? At the risk of being misunderstood, how can we experience this kind of intimacy with Jesus—such a deep closeness with Christ that it practically shines from you wherever you go—subway or sidewalk, conservatory or laboratory, classroom or boardroom, dorm room or family room—wherever you go, the glow of Christ in you?

Because let's be honest—there is simply no other way for the eleventh commandment of Jesus to come true in the life of this community of faith, in the life of any of us.

" 'I give you a new commandment, that you love one another. Just as I have loved you, you also should love one another. By this everyone will know that you are my disciples, if you have love for one another.' "[1]

The only way the world will ever recognize the people of Christ at the end of time will be by the way they love each other and the world around them. Jesus gives no other identifying mark than bold, radical love! So the question begs to be asked:

THE ELEVENTH COMMANDMENT

How can we love—really, truly love others—like Jesus did?

In our last chapter we went backward a few upper-room moments to discover the first key to the eleventh commandment. Now let's turn around and move forward a few moments for the next key to unlocking this forgotten commandment. In fact, let's move forward just far enough to physically move out of the stuffy upper room into the fresh and cool of that springtime midnight.

Most people think that John 13 through 17 all transpired in the upper room that fateful Thursday evening. But in reality, when you put the three synoptic Gospel accounts beside John's Gospel, you discover that only chapters 13 and 14 took place up those stairs. The rest of the red-lettered words of Jesus in chapters 15 through17 were spoken and prayed beneath the full-orbed Passover moon—outdoors. The clue is tucked away in the easy-to-miss last line of chapter 14, where Jesus says to the eleven remaining disciples, " 'Rise, let us be on our way.' "[2] In other words, "Let's go, fellas—it's time to leave."

And so they do—out the wooden door, quietly down the clay stairs into the now-silver shadows of night. Beneath the patches of light and dark, Jesus leads His band of friends through the winding alley and out the eastern gate toward their familiar night haunt across the valley, the Garden of Gethsemane.

One summer I traced their steps from the same Jerusalem upper room, up the alley, out the gate and down the rather steep and bumpy, stony pathway that descends from the wall to a notch in the valley below called the Kidron. Archaeologists tell us there are very few Roman pathways from the time of Christ still existing in modern Jerusalem today. But this one has survived, and scholars believe it was the very path over which the sandals of Jesus picked their way beneath the silver light of the A. D. 31 full Passover moon.

"Abide in Me"

Somewhere along that descending and crooked pathway, the band of twelve passes near a hanging vineyard trellis. For the Master Teacher this moon-bathed moment becomes the perfect setting for a truth He's been waiting to teach His eleven students. Earlier in the evening He had commanded them, "Love one another." He had informed them that such love would be the convincing evidence civilization would need to recognize them as His people. Now at last He is ready with further, vital instructions on the *how to*—how they could love just like He loves.

And so stepping off the pathway and through the silver patches, Jesus reaches for the trellis, lifting up a leafy twist of the vine. Holding the vine in a hand soon to be nail-pierced, Jesus begins to teach:

> "I am the true vine, and my Father is the vinegrower. He removes every branch in me that bears no fruit. Every branch that bears fruit he prunes to make it bear more fruit. You have already been cleansed by the word that I have spoken to you. Abide in me as I abide in you. Just as the branch cannot bear fruit by itself unless it abides in the vine, neither can you unless you abide in me. I am the vine, you are the branches. Those who abide in me and I in them bear much fruit, because apart from me you can do nothing. . . . As the Father has loved me, so I have loved you; abide in my love. . . . This is my commandment, that you love one another as I have loved you."[3]

Every loyal and patriotic Jew loved the vine metaphor! During the time of the Maccabeans, in fact, Israel's coinage bore the stamp of a vine. Israel was God's true vine, they all declared. But tonight Jesus flips that coin right side up with the clarion announcement that tomorrow's Victim on Calvary is the only true Vine that shall ever be. Even as the fruit of the vine is crushed and flows scarlet beneath the silver moon tonight, even so tomorrow the true Vine shall flow with the crimson of life crushed from His broken heart.

"I am the vine, you are the branches." "Abide in me as I abide in you."

Through a solitary metaphor Jesus pours the secrets of eternity into a single teaching. He seizes a word He spoke beneath the orange torches of the upper room, and now ten times in a row He turns the noun into a verb. "In my Father's house are many *mansions*" becomes " '*abide* in me as I *abide* in you.' "[4] These words come from the same Greek root. Which means the translation could also read, "Mansion in Me and I will mansion in you." Or, "Take up residence in Me, as I take up residence in you." That's why Eugene Peterson has chosen to translate this line: "Live in me. Make your home in me just as I do in you."[5]

No closer connection

However you wish to express it, Jesus' dynamic midnight teaching is clear—He is offering every friend and follower an intimacy of relationship and a union so close it can be likened only to the bonded connection between a living branch and the life-giving vine. "I am the vine, you are the branches." There can be no closer or more intimate connection!

Oswald Chambers describes it with these words: "It is a joy to Jesus when a disciple takes time to step more intimately with Him. Fruit bearing is always mentioned as the manifestation of an intimate union with Jesus Christ." "The whole discipline of life is to enable us to enter into this closest relationship with Jesus Christ."[6]

Jesus pours all of eternity and "the whole discipline of life" into this green-and-purple metaphor. So close is the friendship He is offering that Jesus actually describes it as blossoming into succulent fruit. " 'Those who abide in me and I in them bear much fruit.' " What kind of fruit? " 'That you love one another as I have loved you.' "[7]

We are nothing apart from Him

It doesn't take a botanist or a horticulturist to know that the sole object of a branch's connection to the vine is for the sake of growing fruit! Branches exist for no other purpose. They live to bear fruit. Only in an Aesop's fable would you read of a branch that severed itself from the vine and ran away from home to bear fruit on its own. Severed branches are dead branches.

" 'Because apart from me you can do nothing.' "[8] And to make certain we understand the word "nothing" John inserts a double negative once again. Earlier in the evening Peter had cried out to Jesus (in Greek), "You will *no not* wash my feet!" Now at midnight Jesus cries out to Peter and the rest (in Greek), "Apart from Me you can do *no not* anything!" Like the man quipped, "Which part of 'No' don't you understand—the 'n' or the 'o'?" "Without Me, you can do *no*-thing." Period. *Nada.*

What a radical word to such a self-sufficient postmodern generation! Living as we are in the most individualistic and self-dependent society in history, this new millennial generation has fooled itself into believing it can solve, or at least resolve, the cosmic problems of this sprawling universe. But our own presidential and political fiascos, our own economic and technological meltdowns, our own medical and social epidemics are a nagging reminder that our self-sufficiency is as secure as a stock certificate.

Until we learn this truth—that we are nothing without Jesus—even we who declare our allegiance to Him will never discover the secret to spiritual life and growth. We are nothing without Jesus. "Apart from me you can do nothing." Or expressed in the positive—"I can do all things through him who strengthens me."[9]

Jesus is everything

If only we could grasp this truth—that we are nothing without Jesus, but that we are everything with Him, because *Jesus is everything*—what a freedom to live and to truly love would be ours! If only our daily preoccupation and hourly passion were for Jesus.

The great conductor Arturo Toscanini was rehearsing Beethoven's Ninth Symphony with the New York Philharmonic Orchestra. When the maestro had determined that the orchestra was ready, he directed them through the entire composition without stopping.

After the last note of the symphony's moving finale had echoed away, silence filled the rehearsal hall. Toscanini spoke at last. "Who am I?" he asked. No one answered. "Who is Toscanini? I am nobody!" the maestro's voice echoed through the chamber.

But then with a mighty wave of his outstretched baton, Toscanini exclaimed into the silence, "It is Beethoven—he is everything!"

Until we grasp that truth—that Jesus is everything—we will *never* discover the secret to radiating the love of Jesus to one another and to the world.

A friend of mine shared with me a small pamphlet, "The Life That Wins," written years ago by Charles Trumbull. I have read and reread it numerous times, because it brings such a fresh sense of what Jesus was really saying that midnight beside the vine trellis. As Trumbull wrote:

There is only one life that wins; and that is the life of Jesus Christ. Every man may have that life; every man may live that life. I do not mean that every man may be Christlike; I mean something very much better than that. I do not mean that man may always have Christ's help; I mean something better than that. I do not mean that a man may have power from Christ; I mean something very much better than power. And I do not mean that a man shall be merely saved from his sins and kept from sinning; I mean something better than even that victory.[10]

What is this "something better" that seemed to have turned Trumbull's life around?

Saturated in Christ

Think of the greatest Christians you have ever known? Can you put your finger on an identifiable common denominator to their lives? The more I've reflected on that question, the more I've concluded that in Jesus' midnight injunction—"Abide in me as I abide in you"—is to be found the secret to the passion in the lives of the greatest Christians I have known either personally or have read about biographically. Would you agree?

To a man and woman they lived and demonstrated what we might call the "Christ saturation" of John 15. "Abide in me as I abide in you."

When that dawned on me, I decided to check it out. And so I began to pull down biographies from my own library shelves to examine the experiences of some of the great heroes of faith—Martin Luther, John Wesley, Dwight L. Moody, Hudson Taylor, Oswald Chambers, to name a few. I reread their conversion stories. And there it was—inescapable—as plain as day: the unmistakable "Christ saturation" of their lives. They were all men and women saturated with Jesus!

I went back to the life of the greatest Christian in history—the apostle Paul—and sure enough, there it was, saturating his correspondence and writing. So much so that I grabbed a pocket notebook and began to annotate every verse I could find that exhibited Paul's "Jesus saturation." I now have pages of evidence! As I numbered them one by one, for example, I came to #41, Colossians 3:11—"Christ is all and in all." How could you possibly express the "Christ saturation" more succinctly or powerfully! "Christ is all and in all" — Jesus is everything! Paul was saturated with Jesus.

He and all the rest of those men and women were like a sponge—a plain old kitchen or car wash or bathtub sponge. You know the secret of a sponge, don't you? It is its mysterious (so it seems to my simple mind) ability to absorb and retain water. And not just a little water, mind you, but inordinate amounts of water!

How does the sponge pull off such a grand feat? Apparently, it is filled with hundreds of small empty chambers. When the sponge comes in contact with water, it is the nature of the sponge to immediately begin to absorb that water, chamber by chamber, drop by drop. The longer the sponge is immersed in the water, the more deeply the water is able to penetrate the innermost chambers. Until eventually, the sponge becomes utterly saturated with the water, every chamber filled to the max, every nook and cranny filled to overflowing.

"Abide in me as I abide in you."

Isn't the "Christ saturation" of God's closest friends throughout history like a sponge? Weren't they all men and women who over the years immersed themselves deeper and deeper into the life and love of Jesus? Like thirsty sponges, didn't they keep throwing open every chamber of their hearts and minds and lives until they were "filled with all the fullness of God"?[11] Isn't that why we remember them? Because they became so saturated with the One who is the water of life, that the promise was proved true, " 'Out of the believer's heart shall flow rivers of living water' "?[12]

"Abide in me as I abide in you."

A branch connected and bonded to the vine, a sponge immersed and saturated with water—the truth is, that is the only way the eleventh commandment will ever be lived, let alone kept. " 'This is my commandment, that you love one another as I have loved you.' "[13]

Oh sure, you and I can make our sporadic, anemic stabs at obligatory loving of one another, without being connected or saturated. But—to mix the metaphors—how quickly the branch shrivels and how rapidly the sponge goes dry. The secret, you see, is in the abiding.

A choice we make

"Abide in me as I abide in you." Or as the *New International Version* translates it: " 'Remain in me, and I will remain in you.' " Because in the end it's a choice. A simple choice you and I make at the rising of every new day. Shall I remain in Jesus today? Shall I live with Him, abide with Him through the hours ahead? And shall I invite Him to come and remain with me and live with me this day? The lives of the greatest men and women of faith who ever lived came down to that simple, daily choice. A choice to decide to remain connected, a desire to become saturated.

"Abide in me as I abide in you." The only difference today is that our bookstore shelves are now lined with more how-to-pray-and-study-your-Bible-to-keep-close-to-Jesus books than ever before in history. There is a plethora of devotional strategies waiting for you out there to guide you in your decision and desire to abide in Christ. The door is wide open for any man or woman who longs for "Christ saturation" today.

So what are we waiting for? " 'Listen! I am standing at the door, knocking; if you hear my voice and open the door, I will come in to you.' "[14]

Which being interpreted means, "Abide in me as I abide in you."

As Charles Trumbull wrote: "Jesus Christ does not want to be our helper; He wants to be our life. He does not want us to work for Him. He wants us to let Him do His work through us. When our life is not only Christ's but Christ, our life will be a winning life; for He cannot fail."[15]

Just ask Edwina Humphrey Flynn. She asked Him to abide with her that day. And He came in so deeply they could see His light shining under her door.

" 'By this everyone will know that you are my disciples.' "[16]

Maybe it's time we all opened the door and let Him come in!

---

[1] John 13:34, 35.
[2] John 14:31.
[3] John 15:1-5, 9, 12.
[4] John 14:2, KJV; 15:4.
[5] John 15:4, *The Message.*
[6] Oswald Chambers, *My Utmost for His Highest,* p. 7.
[7] John 15:5, 12.
[8] John 15:5.
[9] Philippians 4:13.
[10] Charles Trumbull, "The Life That Wins," pp. 5, 6.
[11] Ephesians 3:19.
[12] John 7:38.
[13] John 15:12.
[14] Revelation 3:20.
[15] Charles Trumbull, "The Life That Wins," p. 26
[16] John 13:35.

CHOKING ON A CAMEL

Woe to you, scribes and Pharisees, hypocrites! For you tithe mint, dill, and cummin, and have neglected the weightier matters of the law: justice and mercy and faith. It is these you ought to have practiced without neglecting the others. You blind guides! You strain out a gnat, but swallow a camel!'"[1]

Hypocrites!

Are we choking on a camel?

I wish He hadn't called you and me hypocrites, don't you? I don't mind Him calling the Pharisees that; they deserve it! But me? And you? Please!

The fact is, though, that long ago little Greek boys would run up to their mothers and tug on their aprons, "Mama, when I grow up I want to be a hypocrite!"

And the mothers would stoop over and pat them on the head

with a smile, "Good for you, my son. I think you'll make a great hypocrite when you grow up!"

Because the same word we use today had an entirely different meaning long ago. *Hupokrite,* in Greek, was the technical name for Greek actors! So back then Hollywood was filled with hypocrites. That's what they were. The word meant "actor."

You see, Greek actors were very skilled at being able to change their masks and play the role of someone else—two-faced, three-faced, five-faced. It didn't matter. All the actor had to do was change his mask and play another part.

So the conversation could really go something like, "What do you do for a living?"

"Oh, I'm a hypocrite!"

"You are? Wow! Can I have your autograph? I've always wanted the autograph of a hypocrite!"

But obviously over the centuries, slowly but surely, the word began to append to itself negative connotations. So that by the time Jesus uses the word *hupokrite* here in Matthew 23:23, it isn't exactly a compliment! Two-faced, pretentious pretenders. That's what He meant.

I don't mind Him calling the Pharisees hypocrites. But does he have to do it to the church at the dawning of a new millennium? Seven stinging woes He levels against the ecclesiastical hierarchy. But do we have to read them?

No—not all of them. Just one will do for those of us who are brooding upon the eleventh commandment. The fourth woe will be sufficient, I'm sure.

"Woe to you, scribes and Pharisees, hypocrites! For you tithe mint, dill, and cummin, and have neglected the weightier matters of the law: justice and mercy and faith. It is these you ought to have practiced without neglecting the others."[2]

At least he hands out one compliment here! "You tithe."

Is Jesus somehow suggesting that it would be a sin to tithe? Are you kidding! A man would be a fool *not* to invite God to be the senior partner of his financial management. Ditto for a woman. Returning a tenth of your income to God is a radical faith declaration. "God, You own all the silver and gold in this world and the cattle on a thousand hills—and the hills under the cattle. So I return this one-tenth of my income to You. After all, You said, 'Bring all the tithes into the storehouse and prove Me now, test Me now, and see if I will not open to you the windows of heaven that there will not be room enough to receive it.'[3] That's what You said, dear God, and so I return to You Your tithe, believing that You are so sovereign and so great and so good that You will take the 90 percent I have left, and You will stretch it farther than the 100 percent I would have had if I hadn't asked you to be the senior partner in my financial affairs."

Jesus is *not* condemning tithing. After all, He was the One who came up with the idea in the first place long, long ago! Long before they had currency and coins, God declared to the children of Israel that as a sign that they sincerely desired His senior partnership they were to return tithe—of what? "All tithes from the land, whether the seed from the ground or the fruit from the tree, are the Lord's; they are holy to the Lord."[4]

The devout Jews in the time of Jesus knew that. Which is why some of them were even tithing the small herb gardens they grew out back to spice up their foods. Jesus is *not* condemning their scrupulous efforts to faithfully return to God a tenth of their increase.

People come to me and ask, "Pastor, should I tithe my cash gifts? Should I tithe my allowance? Should I tithe my income tax refunds? Should I tithe my investments?"

Jesus is *not* saying No, No, No to all those questions. He isn't back-pedaling God's profound offer to be our senior partner. My response to those who inquire—"How much of my finances should I ask God to manage?"—is plain and simple: Let Him have controlling interest in everything you own, because you'll never have a wiser and more competent and more successful investment manager! Charles Schwab isn't bad, but God is great!

Weightier matters

"Woe to you, scribes and Pharisees, hypocrites! For you tithe mint, dill, and cummin, and have neglected the weightier matters of the law: justice and mercy and faith. It is these you ought to have practiced without neglecting the others."

Did you catch His words, "The weightier matters of the law"? Does that come as a surprise to you, as it does to some others? That when it comes to God's revealed Word and will, there are some matters weightier, heavier, more important than others?

Jesus clearly reveals here the existence of a hierarchy of values and truths within the corpus of God's revealed will, His law. As important as tithing is, there are "weightier matters of the law." And what are they?

"Woe to you, scribes and Pharisees, hypocrites! For you tithe mint, dill, and cummin, and have neglected the weightier matters of the law: justice and mercy and faith. It is these you ought to have practiced without neglecting the others."

The three "weightier matters of the law" that Christ identifies are justice, mercy, and faith. And what is justice? It is "rightness" between you and me. Justice has to do with human relationships—it clearly deals with the *horizontal* (human-to-human) dimension of living.

What is mercy? It is "compassion" between you and me. It, too, has much to do with human relationships; it also clearly deals with the *horizontal* dimension of living.

And what is faith? Luke in his parallel account of this passage records it as " 'the love of God.' "[5] Clearly, this weightier matter of the law captures the *vertical* dimension of life—our human-to-God relationship.

But please note it carefully: Two out of the three weightier matters of the law that Jesus identifies have to do with our horizontal relationships—our human-to-human interactions. Is Jesus somehow out of kilter and off balance from the Law and the Prophets? Are you kidding!

What Jesus has just done is take that grand Old Testament declaration of true religion and baptize it into the new covenant. "He has showed you, O man, what is good. And what does the LORD require of you: To act justly and to love mercy and to walk humbly with your God."[6] There they are—justice, mercy, and faith.

Loving God/loving others

Jesus' profound point is inescapable. More important than asking an unseen God to be my senior partner through tithing—as important as that is—is how I treat the human beings I see and meet all around me. I can't see God, but I can sure see them!

In the provocative words of the apostle John: "If anyone says, 'I love God,' yet hates his brother, he is a liar. For anyone who does not love his brother, whom he has seen, cannot love God, whom he has not seen."[7]

" 'Woe to you, scribes and Pharisees, hypocrites! For you tithe mint, dill, and cummin, and have neglected the weightier matters of the law: justice and mercy and faith. It is these you ought to have practiced without neglecting the others. You blind guides! You strain out a gnat, but swallow a camel!' "[8]

How do you choke on a camel? Watch the Pharisees whom Christ is addressing. You see, the smallest unclean creature listed in the dietary code of Leviticus 11 was the gnat, and the largest unclean creature in that same code was the camel. Jesus' stinging hyperbole was based on the practice of the Pharisees to filter their drinks to avoid the ingestion of all unclean bugs. Strict Jews would take a piece of linen or gauze, place it over their cups, and would strain their wine, vinegar, and other potable liquids before drinking.

So there they are—the Pharisees—sipping sanctimoniously from their gnat-filtered cups, and all the while, inside that cup, you can hear and smell and see the splish-splashing of a hairy, big-lipped, hump-backed dromedary.

"Cheers! We got the gnats out!" And as they guzzle their drinks down, they choke on a camel!

Majoring in minors

You blind hypocrites! You major in the minors, and you minor in the majors. You strain out a gnat, but you choke down a camel. You tithe your pennies, but you ignore your neighbors. You say you love the truth, but you refuse to live the truth.

And what is the truth?

> "I give you a new commandment, that you love one another. Just as I have loved you, you also should love one another. By this everyone will know that you are my disciples, if you have love for one another."[9]

> "Woe to you, scribes and Pharisees, hypocrites! For you tithe mint, dill, and cummin, and have neglected the weightier matters of the law: justice and mercy and faith. It is these you ought to have practiced without neglecting the others. You blind guides! You strain out a gnat, but swallow a camel!"[10]

If anyone says, "I love God," yet hates his brother, he is a liar. For anyone who does not love his brother, whom he has seen, cannot love God, whom he has not seen.[11]

We can preach on satellite seminars till we are blue in the face, but if we omit "the weightier matters of the law" we are no better than the scribes and Pharisees. " 'Woe to you, scribes and Pharisees, hypocrites! For you cross sea and land to make a single convert, and you make the new convert twice as much a child of hell as yourselves.' "[12]

We can boast of nationally ranked universities and nationally acclaimed hospitals until we are hoarse, but if we omit "the weightier matters of the law" we are no better than the scribes and Pharisees. " 'Woe to you, scribes and Pharisees, hypocrites! For you are like white-washed tombs, which on the outside look beautiful, but inside they are full of the bones of the dead and all kinds of filth.' "[13]

Jesus' somber warning is clear: If this community of faith does not yet learn how to love one another, the demise of our community and the disintegration of our faith are assured. For we will choke in the end on a camel.

Choking on the camel of racism

Take the hairy, unclean camel of racism, for example.

Let me be even more specific. The Seventh-day Adventist Church in North America at the end of the millennium convened a "Race Summit" at our world headquarters. Representatives from across the continent gathered to consider and confront the issue of racism within this community of faith. Racism in its institutions, racism in its congregations, racism in its administrative and judicatory policies. In short, the delegates gathered to ponder the implications of the eleventh commandment in contemporary Adventism. " 'By this everyone will know that you are my disciples, if you have love for one another,' " Jesus commanded us.[14]

However, He not only commanded us with His words; His very life example remains a living command! For it surely can be argued that Jesus spent His ministry desperately trying to break down the walls of prejudice, the racial and ethnic barriers that had grown up in the hearts of His people.

Witness His treatment of the hated Samaritans. He reserved for a lone woman of that race the most sublime truth He ever uttered. A woman who had three strikes against her: She was a Samaritan, she was a woman, she was an adulteress. And when He struggled to break through the Jewish prejudice and pride by telling a story of merciful compassion, it may have taken gall to make the hero of the story a Samaritan. But it took *chutzpah* to make the Samaritan "good." For the Jews had a saying, "The only good Samaritan is a dead one."

Over and over again—whether it was with the pleading Syro-Phoenecian mother or with the demurring Roman centurion—Jesus cut across social prejudices in a passionate effort to break down the dividing walls.

And on the eve of His bloody death, Jesus appeals one last time to the followers He will leave behind: " 'I give you a new commandment, that you love one another. Just as I have loved you, you also should love one another. By this everyone will know that you are my disciples, if you have love for one another.' "[15]

But two millennia later, have we omitted these "weightier matters of the law"? Are we, too, straining our gnats and swallowing our camels?

Racism, in all its forms, is not only "omitting the weightier matters of the law"; it is a direct assault on the Lawgiver Himself. For if we cannot love those we see, how under heaven shall we ever love the God we cannot see?

Racism and Adventists

Take again the hairy, unclean camel of racism. Racism is no longer about indentured slaves and southern plantations. Racism can rear its hairy, ugly head whenever your lunch table crowd begins its calloused litany of racial and ethnic jokes. Refusing to laugh isn't enough anymore. To oppose racism is to speak up on the spot in protest—whether it's to a committee joke or a coffee-break story. The ones who are silent are choking on a camel. (No wonder they can't speak!)

The ugly, hairy head of the racism camel can rear itself in the hiring and firing procedures where you work or where you go to school. And you can spot it in committee and board composi-tions. The absence of racial representation is often thunderous in its silence. Somebody is going to have to stand up and speak out. Or will you choke on that camel?

And then there is the matter of regional conferences in the Seventh-day Adventist Church in North America—these "separate-but-equal" divisions of administrative and congrega-tional organization. They have a long and justifiable history to offset the wrongs and inequities of the past.

But are they fast becoming a hairy and peculiar Adventist anomaly in our society? How shall we explain to a new genera-tion of young that while there is no such thing as a White IBM and a Black IBM or a White Ford Motors and a Black Ford Mo-tors, there are still such things as White Adventist conferences and Black Adventist conferences in the same America? If sepa-rate-but-equal facilities and organizations are so productive in the third millennium, why don't the Fortune 500 companies of America all divide into racial administrative units? And if reli-gion is somehow exempted from the social norms of a progres-sive society, then why have other American denominations abandoned their racial divisions and united in ecclesiastical solidarity?

If we, as White Adventists, choose to hide behind "regional conferences" as a separate-but-equal judicatory provision so that "they" can have the feeling of being "president" and "administrators"—as long as "they" aren't "our" presidents and administrators—then are we not spiritually choking to death on a camel? For Christianity is always doomed when it attempts to segregate itself into separate-but-equal camps. Calvary is antithetical to such a brand of religion and racism.

And if we, as Black Adventists, choose to hide behind "regional conferences" as being a matter of "our rights and our authority and our own power base" within the community of faith, then are we not, too, spiritually choking to death on a camel? For Christianity is always doomed when it seeks to exert itself through a clamoring for rights and power. Calvary is antithetical to such a brand of religion and racism.

At this dawning of a new millennium hasn't the time come for the establishment of single conferences for each geographic region? Isn't it time for "a new creation in Christ" of united conferences and united congregations and a united people with a united mission and a united love for a lost and disunited world?

I know what the classic response to such an appeal has been: "Well, you just don't understand how complicated this matter is. If you only knew the history of regional conferences, you would understand why we must continue to cling to them for representation and/or for separation." But if we consistently used that kind of smoke-screen logic appealing to history, we'd all be indentured slaves on some feudal lord's plantation or estate. To appeal to the past as an ironclad template for the future condemns us to wander in the wilderness for generations to come. At some point a new generation must arise and lead us across the Jordan!

Enough is enough

Perhaps it is to the young we need to be appealing, these who comprise the most color-blind generation in the history of this nation and this Church. Maybe we must wait for one last generation to be buried in the sands this side of Canaan, so that the young in Christ might rise up and declare to their elders, "Enough is enough. Neither corporate nor religious America tolerates a separate-but-equal racial division. It is high time for the Church to refuse to do so, as well!"

USA Weekend magazine ran a cover story on two Baptist churches in St. Paul, Minnesota—one Black, one White—that also came to that "enough is enough" moment. It is a story of love triumphing over cultural and racial differences. It isn't a story about racial integration. Instead it is a wonderful narrative about racial reconciliation. And there is a difference:

> Racial reconciliation is not the same as integration. The latter removes formal barriers, primarily laws, that keep people apart, but leaves intact the centuries-old images, beliefs, and cultural barriers that divide people— the miles-high walls in our hearts and minds. In racial reconciliation, individuals consciously strive to overcome the legacy of racism, first by forging genuine bonds with at least one person of a different race.[16]

It is *not* a complicated matter. What is so difficult about the Whites and Blacks of the Adventist Church coming together and confessing that we have *all* been guilty of racism? That we are all still choking on the hairy, unclean camel of racism? But that enough is enough!

Isn't it clear that God isn't looking for a White church or a Black church? He waits for the remnant church. "By this will the world know that you are My people, if you have love for one another."

Radical love

When a person is choking to death, what can save him is called the Hiemlich maneuver. If you see someone choking or making the universal sign of choking (a hand to the throat), act quickly and you may become his savior. First, come behind him, then put your arms around him, cup your hands into a fist, squeezing them tightly beneath his rib cage, followed by a quick sharp thrust inward and upward. By expelling the obstructing foreign matter within the victim, the Hiemlich maneuver is truly a life-saving action.

There is a similar maneuver that can also save a church found choking on a camel. Call it the Hiemlich maneuver of Calvary, if you will. It's that saving moment when in desperation we, the Church, cast ourselves upon the crucified One, allowing Him to embrace us, His arms around us, His nail-scarred hands pressed so tightly against us that what is choking us to death is expelled at last. The Hiemlich maneuver of Calvary.

What else can save our suffocating church on this continent? How else will it finally dawn upon our choking hearts that—"red and yellow, black and white"—we are, all of us, *already* loved so deeply by our Father that there is no need any longer to cling to our racial insecurities. What else but the Cross can unchain us from the slavery of our stubborn and destructive pride?

Only the radical love of Christ through the Hiemlich-like embrace of Calvary can expel the deadly and unclean camel of racism.

As Ephesians 2 so powerfully declares: "But now in Christ Jesus, you who were once far off have been brought near by the blood of Christ. For he is our peace; in his flesh he has made both groups into one and has broken down the dividing wall, that is, the hostility between us . . . that he might . . . reconcile both groups to God in one body through the cross, thus putting to death that hostility through it."[17]

Let the hypocrites choke on their camels.

But let the black and brown and white and yellow hands of Adventism tear down the wall Christ died to obliterate two millennia ago.

Can you think of a more compelling demonstration of the eleventh commandment in the third millennium?

" 'I give you a new commandment, that you love one another. Just as I have loved you, you also should love one another. By this everyone will know that you are my disciples, if you have love for one another.' "[18]

---

1. Matthew 23:23, 24.
2. Matthew 23:23.
3. See Malachi 3:10.
4. Leviticus 27:30.
5. Luke 11:42.
6. Micah 6:8, NIV.
7. 1 John 4:20, NIV.
8. Matthew 23:23, 24.
9. John 13:34, 35.
10. Matthew 23:23, 24.
11. 1 John 4:20, NIV.
12. Matthew 23:15.
13. Matthew 23:27.
14. John 13:35.
15. John 13:34, 35.
16. *USA Weekend*, September 10-12, 1999, p. 6.
17. Ephesians 2:13, 14, 16.
18. John 13:34, 35.

I *give you
a new commandment,
that you love one another.
Just as I have loved you,
you also should love
one another.'"*

JOHN 13:34

CHAPTER 5

"CALLED TO HATE?"

Called to hate?" That headline to a "special news report" in *Christianity Today* caught my eye. As did the stunning picture posted beside it. I read on:

> After gay student Matthew Shepard was beaten to death in October 1998, a tall man in a white cowboy hat descended upon the Wyoming funeral waving fluorescent signs of Shepard's face amid blood-red flames and chanting the mantra "Matt is in hell."[1]

On the opposite page appeared a full-color, full-page photograph of self-proclaimed preacher and pastor Fred Phelps. Standing by the side of a road, garbed in what has become his trademark white cowboy hat, wrap-around sunglasses, and dark blue dress suit—there he was with a white-gloved hand resting against his giant homemade U.S. flag-draped wooden sign that proclaimed to all who passed by: "Fags are worthy of death—Romans 1:32."

Speaking on the record to a reporter, Fred Phelps was inflexible: "God won't allow us to have excuses. . . . Some are called to preach his message of love, and I've been called to preach his message of hate. Where are the old-time preachers who tell people the truth? God hates evildoers and fornicators and fags."[2]

Did I read and hear him correctly? He's been called to preach God's "message of hate"? How and where on earth could Phelps have ever heard such a call?

> Understanding Fred Phelps means understanding the call he received to be a latter-day prophet. That call, he says, came at a sweltering tent meeting in Meridian, Mississippi, when the elders of his church gathered around him to anoint him, using the words of Isaiah 58:1: "Shout it aloud, do not hold back. Raise your voice like a trumpet. Declare to my people their rebellion and to the house of Jacob their sins." [And so] when Phelps takes the pulpit at Westboro Baptist Church in Topeka, Kansas, sin is usually a large part of the sermon.[3]

Can you believe it? Poor Fred Phelps, who thinks he's been called to preach the message, "God hates sinners," to a dying world already packed to its gills and walls with sinners the likes of you and me! And it would surely be a comedy were it not such a tragedy—Phelps's conviction that Isaiah 58:1 is divine license for his call to hate.

A message to God's people

If only he had taken the time to read that dusty ancient passage, he would have discovered that in fact it is precisely *the very opposite call!*

But is Phelps alone in his mistaken interpretation? I squirm a bit to confess that there are preachers much closer to home who have also championed Isaiah 58's opening salvo to justify their own "tough stance" on sin and sinners in the church. Kind of like the fabled retort of President Calvin Coolidge upon returning from attending church one morning. When asked by his wife what the preacher preached about, Coolidge struggled to recall the message, and finally replied, "Sin."

"And what about sin?" she persisted.

The president retorted, "He was against it."

But then, who isn't?

But is Isaiah 58:1 really God's call to preach a message of hate? Or is it, instead, His passionate appeal to both preach and practice the very opposite? Examine the ancient scroll for yourself:

> Shout out, do not hold back! Lift up your voice like a trumpet! Announce to my people their rebellion, to the house of Jacob their sins. Yet day after day they seek me and delight to know my ways, as if they were a nation that practiced righteousness and did not forsake the ordinance of their God; they ask of me righteous judgments, they delight to draw near to God. "Why do we fast, but you do not see? Why humble ourselves, but you do not notice?"[4]

One reality is immediately clear from even a cursory reading of this chapter: God certainly isn't calling His people to hurry out into the world and there proclaim and preach the sins *of* the world *to* the world. Because Isaiah 58:1 clearly is not the *mission of the church* to the world—it is rather the *message of God* to the church! And therein lies a very major difference.

It's as if God is putting His arm around His friend and prophet Isaiah and pleading with him: "Isaiah, you've got to help Me get the attention of My people. They have it all wrong and all backwards! They keep trying to remind Me that they have the truth, the truth, the truth. But Isaiah, you must cry it out in no uncertain terms: 'You've lost the truth, the truth, the truth!' "

That is what Isaiah 58 is about—how a people who once upon a time were entrusted with "the truth" have lost it and how in the end they can yet recover it.

What truth?

A "Day of Atonement" appeal

Before God answers that question, it is intriguing to spot the unmistakable clues and code words tucked inside Isaiah 58 that reveal who the intended audience is to be: a people living in the midst of the Day of Atonement! Nobody talks much about it anymore, but you do remember the ancient holy day Yom Kippur, don't you? Our Jewish friends still celebrate that Day of Atonement every autumn. For ancient Israel it came once a year as a sober symbol and somber reminder that God would convene a day of judgment at the end of time to finally and strategically "cleanse" this world of sin. But in the midst of its sobering wake-up call, the Day of Atonement was, and is, a glad and passionate invitation from God to His friends on earth to become "at-one" at last with Him! Isaiah 58 shoots like an arrow straight into the heart of a people living in that Day of At-one-ment.

Which may be all the more reason, Fred Phelps aside, for you and me to pay particularly close attention to this ancient appeal from God.

What makes this a "Day of Atonement" appeal? "Lift up your voice like a trumpet," God cries out to Isaiah in verse one. The Hebrew word for trumpet here is *shophar*. When I strolled the alleyways of Jerusalem a few summers ago, shops everywhere were offering these *shophars* for sale—the long, twisted ram horns that have traditionally been blown over the millennia (blasted, really, is how it sounded to me!) as calls to worship or signals of warning. It was the *shophar* that was used to herald the arrival of the Day of Atonement. The psalmist exclaims: "Blow the trumpet [*shophar*] at the new moon, at the full moon, on our festal day."[5] When those piercing, melancholy wails were heard echoing across the community of faith, all knew that the festal Day had arrived— it was "at-one-ment" time.

But there is more Day of Atonement language in Isaiah 58. In verse 3 the people cry out to God, " 'Why do we fast, but you do not see?' " Interestingly enough, the Day of Atonement was the only day upon which the law required fasting. The *shophar* has announced Yom Kippur's arrival. And in keeping with the Day of Atonement, the people have begun their requisite fasting—dutifully denying themselves some of life's simple pleasures in order to demonstrate their holy commitment to God.

Why doesn't God draw near?

But something's not right; something's gone wrong. They don't seem—or so they complain—to be getting through to God! " 'Why do we fast, but you do not see? Why humble ourselves, but you do not notice?' "[6] Come on, God! We're going through all the proper Day of Atonement motions; but You're not noticing us. What's the matter?

After all, these are good "adventist" people. God Himself describes them as a people who "seem eager" for God to come near them.[7] The Hebrew of that phrase can be translated, "they delight in the drawing near of Elohim [an Old Testament name for God]." That is, they are a people who eagerly keep hoping that the end is near and that God is coming soon! After all, this *is* the Day of Atonement, the great day of judgment. So, for the life of them, they can't figure out why on earth God isn't "drawing near" and coming back to earth with judgments against the lost world! "They ask of me righteous judgments."[8] "Come on, God! We've got the truth; You've got the judgments! What are You waiting for?" is the cry of a people impatiently awaiting the advent of God.

The startling remainder of Isaiah 58 is God's astounding answer to that single query: What are you waiting for?

> Look, you serve your own interest on your fast day, and oppress all your workers. Look, you fast only to quarrel and to fight and to strike with a wicked fist. Such fasting as you do today will not make your voice heard on high.
>
> Is such the fast that I choose, a day to humble oneself? Is it to bow down the head like a bulrush, and to lie in sackcloth and ashes? Will you call this a fast, a day acceptable to the LORD?[9]

Neglecting the weightier matters

God minces no words, as with a wave of His celestial hand He pushes aside their boasted orthodoxy. For here is a religious community obsessed with its religious behavior and ODing (overdosing) on its spiritual disciplines. They have occupied themselves ad nauseam with themselves—with their own praying and fasting and "devotionalizing" and worshiping and "sabbathing." And all the while—as God is about to announce—they have neglected the weightier matters of the law, justice and mercy and faith!

In fact so unbalanced have they become that earlier in this same book God erupted in utter frustration:

> What to me is the multitude of your sacrifices? says the LORD. I have had enough of burnt offerings of rams and the fat of fed beasts; I do not delight in the blood of bulls, or of lambs, or of goats.
>
> When you come to appear before me, who asked this from your hand? Trample my courts no more; bringing offerings is futile; incense is an abomination to me. New moon and sabbath and calling of convocation—I cannot endure solemn assemblies with iniquity. Your new moons and your appointed festivals my soul hates; they have become a burden to me.[10]

Simply put, God bluntly and passionately cries out, *Stop it!* Or as my teenage daughter would say, "Take a chill pill." How could God be any more emphatic with a people obsessed with their peculiar orthodoxies and their practiced observances? Quit playing church! Because I'm sick and tired of being sick and tired of your going through the motions but leaving out the mission!

The "eleventh-commandment" mission

So what's changed over the millennia? Going through the motions? Or leaving out the mission? In the end (and before the end) what would God see changed in the hearts of His community of faith?

God is quick with the answer:

> Is not this the fast that I choose: to loose the bonds of injustice, to undo the thongs of the yoke, to let the op-

pressed go free, and to break every yoke? Is it not to share your bread with the hungry, and bring the homeless poor into your house; when you see the naked, to cover them, and not to hide yourself from your own kin?[11]

What you have just read is the eleventh-commandment mission of the church *in* the end and *before* the end. You may read the Scriptures from cover to cover and you will find no more compelling case for proactive social action than here in Isaiah 58! It is a divine call for the community of faith to immerse itself in the suffering life of the world around it—the hungry, the poor, the homeless, the naked. And not only to immerse itself, but to give of itself to fill those gnawing needs.

Ponder this pointed but practical application of Isaiah 58:

In all our work the principle of unselfishness revealed in Christ's life is to be carried out. Upon the walls of our homes, the pictures, the furnishings, we are to read, "Bring the poor that are cast out to thy house." On our wardrobes we are to see written, as with the finger of God, "Clothe the naked." In the dining room, on the table laden with abundant food, we should see traced, "Is it not to deal thy bread to the hungry?" Isaiah 58:7.[12]

I remind you that the divine appeal of Isaiah 58 throbs with Day of Atonement imagery. That in itself makes this ancient chapter a very contemporary and clarion call from God to a people, His people, living in "the hour of his judgment."[13]

The issue in the judgment

Apparently social action has much to do with the final judgment!

Notice carefully the categories of human misery and need God identifies here in Isaiah 58:6, 7—the hungry, the homeless, the poor, the naked. Do they sound familiar? Do you remember a story Jesus told once upon a time that took these very categories of the socially disenfranchised, the economically marginalized, and the spiritually alienated and wove them into His grand finale parable?

Christ told the story just hours before His crucifixion—the Matthew 25 parable about the King who returns to earth in the end and gathers all the world's children before Him. And even as a good Palestinian shepherd separates the light-haired sheep from the dark-coated goats—sending the sheep in one direction and the goats in another (the goats being voracious eaters, who unless separated could eat the sheep out of house and home!), even so the returning King divides His subjects into two separate camps. And to those gathered at His right hand the Shepherd King announces:

> " 'Come, you that are blessed by my Father, inherit the kingdom prepared for you from the foundation of the world; for I was hungry and you gave me food, I was thirsty and you gave me something to drink, I was a stranger and you welcomed me, I was naked and you gave me clothing, I was sick and you took care of me, I was in prison and you visited me.' "[14]

And when the friends of the Shepherd King hear His commendation, they are utterly non-plused. In humble disbelief they ask Him when in all their days had they even once seen their beloved but far-away King?

"And the king will answer them, 'Truly [amen in the Greek—adding a note of surety and solemnity] I tell you, just as you did it to one of the least of these who are members of my family, you did it to me.' "[15]

Knowing versus showing

Mark it well: The Day of Atonement pronouncement by God in Isaiah 58 is matched by the Day of Judgment pronouncement by Jesus in Matthew 25. And both verdicts are based upon how the socially disenfranchised and the economically marginalized were treated in this life.

Note it carefully: On that day the question will not be: Did you *know* the truth about Me? The question, instead, will be asked: Did you *show* the truth about Me? Both passages powerfully phrase the final question in the judgment: What did you do for those desperately in need—socially, physically, economically?

Still not convinced that our judgment will turn on how we've treated the needy? Then let *The Desire of Ages* weigh in with Isaiah and Jesus in phrasing the final judgment's probing question:

> Thus [with the parable of the sheep and the goats] Christ on the Mount of Olives pictured to His disciples the scene of the great judgment day. And He represented its decision as *turning upon one point*. When the nations are gathered before Him, there will be but two classes, and *their eternal destiny will be determined by what they have done or have neglected to do for Him in the person of the poor and suffering*.[16]

Did you catch that? "Turning upon one point." Not three points or two points or even twenty-seven points. But one point. And what will that single point be? The final query will not be: Did you *know* the truth about Me? The final probing question instead will be: Did you *show* the truth about Me to the socially disenfranchised, the economically marginalized, the spiritually alienated? Did you show My truth by living My love for "the poor and suffering"?

Which means, dear "Day-of-Atonement-Adventist" heart, it is entirely possible that on that day when the children of earth are lined up before the great judgment bar of God, that you will be a few persons back in the line from Mother Teresa. (Allow me this short parable, please.) You remember her, of course, that small frail woman beloved by the world for her compassionate ministry to Calcutta's gutter people—the infectious lepers, the dirt poor, the social dregs and outcasts. (Someone once quipped—it will be a sad, sad day if you're standing behind Mother Teresa at the judgment and you hear God say to her, "You could have done more!")

Judging Mother Teresa

But in this mini-parable let's say that on the great Day of Judgment she actually happens to be just a few people ahead of you in line. On the authority of Isaiah 58 and Matthew 25 and *The Desire of Ages,* it is possible—is it not—that the Judge of heaven will look favorably into the eyes and heart of this little woman who unselfishly lived out the truth of divine love for the most marginalized and disenfranchised people on earth? It is possible—is it not—that though she did not *know* all the truth you do, she in fact *showed* all the truth Jesus did? It is possible—is it not—that in harmony with the pointed observation of *The Desire of Ages,* Mother Teresa's unselfish love for "the poor and suffering" will be the basis upon which her "eternal destiny will be determined"?

To suggest otherwise is to deny the throbbing judgment-day appeal of both Isaiah 58 and Matthew 25.

But back to the mini-parable for a moment. Were you or I to be standing a few places back in that line when Mother Teresa is welcomed with the words, "Come, you blessed of the Lord," it really wouldn't do for us to begin whistling and shouting and holding up seven fingers (on behalf of the seventh-day Sabbath, of course!) for the Judge to see, now would it? Because apparently all the seven-fingered reminders in the world will not override or overrule the Judge's passionate bottom line in His final judgment: Did you love and care for those in need?

And why would the Judge be so passionate about *that?* Because "by this the whole world will know that you are My people, if you have love for one another."[17] Because "in as much as you loved the least of these, you have loved Me."[18] After all, "how can you say you love God, whom you have never seen, when you refuse to love your brother or sister whom you constantly see?"[19]

The evidence is incontrovertible. The radical bottom line of the last judgment is the passionate opening line of the eleventh commandment: " 'I give you a new commandment, that you love one another.' "[20]

Because, you see, Fred Phelps's message—God bless his mistaken soul—is wrong. And Mother Teresa's mission—may she rest in peace—is right. Called to hate? God forbid! The only way through the final judgment is the Judge's call to love: " 'Truly I tell you, just as you did it to one of the least of these who are members of my family, you did it to me.' "[21] And who better to do it to and to do it for than Calvary's Judge and King?

Fred Pratt Green composed this prayer for a judgment-bound church:

When the church of Jesus shuts its outer door,
Lest the roar of traffic drown the voice of prayer,

May our prayers, Lord, make us ten times more aware
That the world we banish is our Christian care.

If our hearts are lifted where devotion soars
High above this hungry suffering world of ours,
Lest our hymns should drug us to forget its needs,
Forge our Christian worship into Christian deeds.

Lest the gifts we offer, money, talents, time,
Serve to salve our conscience to our secret shame,
Lord, reprove, inspire us by the way You give.
Teach us, dying Savior, how true Christians live.[22]

1. *Christianity Today,* October 25, 1999, p. 89.
2. Ibid., p. 90.
3. Ibid.
4. Isaiah 58:1-3.
5. Psalm 81:3.
6. Isaiah 58:3.
7. Isaiah 58:2, NIV.
8. Ibid.
9. Isaiah 58:3-5.
10. Isaiah 1:11-14.
11. Isaiah 58:6, 7.
12. *The Ministry of Healing,* p. 206.
13. Revelation 14:7.
14. Matthew 25:34-36.
15. Matthew 25:40.
16. *The Desire of Ages,* p. 637, emphasis supplied.
17. See John 13:35.
18. See Matthew 25:40.
19. See 1 John 4:20.
20. John 13:34.
21. Matthew 25:40.
22. *Seventh-day Adventist Hymnal,* No. 581.

I *give you*

a new commandment,

that you love one another.

Just as I have loved you,

you also should love

one another.' "

JOHN 13:34

CHAPTER

6

ER

Thanks to NBC television's dramatic hit series, "ER," most everybody these days has been thoroughly inducted into the drama and inner trauma of a county hospital's emergency room. Cook County Hospital in the city of Chicago, to be specific. Not to be outdone, NBC's competitor, CBS, has also weighed in with its own hospital drama, it too set in the Windy City—this one called "Chicago Hope." (I guess Hollywood got tired of L.A., and we in the Midwest got the luck of the draw two hours away in Chicago.)

A great truth about emergency rooms

Be that as it may, now that the nation has become thoroughly acclimated to the inner workings of ER's and hospitals, I'd like to share with you one of the great truths about emergency rooms and hospitals that I have learned. You don't have to watch TV to learn this truth. And I didn't learn it because I am a physician or a surgeon or a nurse (though I'm married to a wonderful nurse) or a lab or X-ray tech or respiratory or physical therapist. I am not medical in any sense or shape of the word (for which you can be quite thankful!). But I have learned this truth, because as a part of my own life calling I have been in many an emergency room and hospital.

The truth? *Emergency rooms and hospitals are messy places.*

Do you know why? Because people come to them in the middle of a crisis. Step into an ER, and you might experience the coagulating odors of vomit and urine and blood and Lysol and antibacterial antiseptics and exotic medicines—all wafting together in the frenetic air of that saving place. Just a few moments earlier those gurneys and beds had been draped with gloriously clean and white and sterile sheets, surrounded by sparkling clean and white and sterile walls and floors and drapes. But in a split second, that sterile white becomes ugly and dirty and splattered and contaminated. But that's OK, because everybody that works and lives in a hospital knows: "This is why we exist; this is why we are here. To get dirtied and bloodied and stained and exposed, while we scramble as a team to save another life."

Oh yes, I have learned the truth about ER's and hospitals: They are messy places. And if I read my Bible aright, the church of Christ is to be the same—a soiled and stained, and at times smelly, saving place for people in the midst of crisis, who come just as they are in desperate hope of being saved and healed before it's too late. If I read my Bible aright, Christ has called His church to become a hospital for sinners.

Matthew's party

The neighborhood hadn't seen so many stretch limos in all

its life! Limousines of every color and hue and size and shape were lined up and down the sidewalks for blocks. (When our son Kirk was a boy and we'd drive over to Chicago, one of his favorite backseat pastimes was to see how many of them he could count—those black and white and silver and grey stretch limos whizzing to and from O'Hare Airport.)

Because stretch limos are a dead giveaway, aren't they? They're rented either for people who are important, or by people who think they are and are trying hard to prove the point. Either way, limousines always catch your eye. So you can imagine the scene they made in that sleepy neighborhood that evening. The place was jammed.

Tonight, though, there are no *paparazzi* in sight. Which is a bit strange, since those ever-present stalking, gawking cameramen would usually crash a party like this one. But not tonight. Because nobody really important is expected . . . in spite of the limos.

And so they arrive in their rented status symbols, men with cheap wrinkled tuxedos and greasy slicked-back hair, each guest with a pasty, gaudy girlfriend clinging to his arm. Limo after limo pulls up to curb. But still no sight of the guest of honor for whom the party is being thrown in the first place.

At last a battered old Plymouth Valiant chugs up the street and into the driveway. And out the guest steps. No tux, no girl, just a K-Mart blue-light special for a suit. But you'd have thought he was the president of the United States, the way the evening's host came bounding down the stairs to welcome his guest, a yellow disposable Kodak snapshot camera flashing away.

Now the party can begin!

After this [Jesus] went out and saw a tax collector named Levi [Matthew], sitting at the tax booth; and he said to him, "Follow me." And he got up, left everything, and followed him.

Then Levi gave a great banquet for him in his house [that evening in that sleepy neighborhood]; and there was a large crowd of tax collectors and others sitting at the table with them. The Pharisees and their scribes were complaining to his disciples, saying, "Why do you eat and drink with tax collectors and sinners?"[1]

Party poopers! As that old jingle chants, "Every party has a pooper—that's why we invited you—party pooper, party pooper!" Because though they weren't invited, they showed up anyway. Probably on foot! The religious hierarchy of Matthew's home town couldn't stomach the thought that Jesus, the popular young Teacher and Healer of Galilee, would show up at the hated tax collector's gaudy, ostentatious manor. But neither would they swallow their pride and invite Him to their villas. So they decided to crash Matt's party. Party poopers.

But I love this Kodak-moment picture of Jesus, don't you? The haughty religious prelates refuse to enter the residence of so "unclean" a sinner as this Roman collaborator tax collector. So I imagine they gather instead beneath one of Matthew's open windows, from which spills the festive light and party cacophony of music and laughter and loud conversations.

Hissing through the window, the Pharisees manage to get the attention of some of the young men who call Jesus Master. Too chicken to pick on Jesus, they turn on His disciples.

"What's the problem with you guys? Don't you realize you're sitting in there eating and drinking with sinners! Are you crazy?"

Who needs the doctor?

And like a good mother or protective father who can be across the room caught up in one conversation but all the while with an ear cocked to monitor the children across the way, Jesus—though He was hardly the one being addressed—interrupts that intended conversation in mid-sentence. Hooray for Jesus! He'll never leave you alone to be trapped by a wily foe.

"Jesus answered, 'Those who are well have no need of a physician, but those who are sick; I have come to call not the righteous but sinners to repentance.' "[2]

There it is as clear as the moon above that evening party. Jesus came to earth for a single reason and a solitary passion: to spend His days and nights with sinners. The ER Physician of the universe didn't descend to our planet to hobnob with the healthy; He came to heal the sick.

Then doesn't it follow that any church that follows Him will do the same? Aren't we to be a hospital for sinners?

What kind of sinners?

I don't see any expressed limitations in Jesus' rejoinder that evening, do you? "I have come to call sinners to repentance." He, therefore, must mean all kinds of sinners. You know the types. Heterosexual sinners and homosexual sinners. Ethical sinners and unethical sinners. Alcoholic sinners and nonalcoholic sinners. Democratic sinners and Republican sinners—and Independents too. Addicted sinners and nonaddicted sinners. Incarcerated sinners and respectable sinners. White sinners and black sinners and brown sinners and yellow sinners. Rich sinners and poor sinners. Young sinners and old sinners. Male sinners and female sinners. Christian sinners and non-Christian sinners. Adventist sinners and non-Adventist sinners. You know the types. *All sinners.*

Apparently, there is no limitation on the kinds of sinners that the church is to be an emergency room for and a hospital to, because Jesus simply said, "I have come to call sinners."

A criticism to covet

Because, let's face it, that's the way Jesus was. He never met a sinner He didn't like or didn't love. In fact what the Pharisees hissed through that open party window about Jesus' disciples they directly aimed straight at Him on another occasion: "Now all the tax collectors [the King James translation calls them "publicans"—not to be confused with Republicans!] and sinners were coming near to listen to [Jesus]. And the Pharisees and the scribes were grumbling and saying, 'This fellow welcomes sinners and eats with them.' "[3]

What a criticism to covet! Wouldn't it be wonderful if they said that about you and me, too? "This man, this woman, welcomes sinners and eats with them." Better yet, what if they said that about our church! "This church welcomes sinners and eats with them." Sadly, I do know some churches that welcome sinners and *eat them!* Which isn't what Jesus ever had in mind for the church, you can be sure.

As long as we're coveting the charges leveled against our Lord once upon a time, there's one more we might add to our list. Jesus noted their criticism of Him on another occasion, when He exposed the typical two-facedness of hypocritical religion, where—as they say—you're damned if you do and damned if you don't. " 'For John the Baptist has come eating no bread and drinking no wine, and you say, "He has a demon;" the Son of Man has come eating and drinking, and you say, "Look, a glutton and a drunkard, *a friend of tax collectors and sinners!*" ' "[4]

What an indictment to covet! What a description of Jesus' church on earth—"a friend of sinners!" But is it a user-friendly description of your home church or mine?

The church is an emergency room and a hospital for sinners.

Have you ever heard of an ER that requires its patients to get cleaned up *before* they show up? Can you imagine that? "Excuse me, ambulance driver! I know we're rushing to the hospital because I'm in bad shape, but I can't go in there looking like this. So would you mind pulling over while I put on my make-up? Thank you. I need a little more light here. After all, I don't want to show up at the hospital looking bad!"

Are you crazy? You're *supposed* to show up looking and feeling bad, or you wouldn't belong in the hospital!

"Excuse me, sir! I need to go back in the house and change my pajamas and blow dry my hair. Then we can rush to the ER and take care of this heart attack of mine."

Are you crazy? There isn't a hospital or ER in the world that requires you to clean yourself and heal yourself before they'll admit you! You're supposed to come just as you are. ERs and hospitals and churches are supposed to be messy places, because people keep showing up in the middle of a life-threatening crisis. That's the whole point!

Museum or hospital?

And yet—I know you won't believe this—there are some people inside the hospital called "the church" who really do believe that people who aren't clean and healthy and sterile like they are, don't belong in that hospital. Now isn't that downright asinine? Some people actually believe that Christ intended for the church to be a museum for saints, rather than a hospital for sinners.

"Oh come on, pastor, we all know the 'remnant church' is to preserve truth and defend orthodoxy—not water it down with insipid, infected, sinner-friendly ways."

Which must be why, like a good museum, some churches keep their treasures behind cold glass, so their teachings won't become contaminated by the warm, messy, soiled, and infected fingers of those who don't belong.

"But don't you know, pastor, that the 'remnant' are to be the called-out ones—we're called to preserve the great truths of God in sterile, separated, germ-free enclaves. After all, what do Revelation 12 and Revelation 14 teach us?"

Well, since you brought it up, let's look up these chapters! Revelation 12:17 reads: "Then the dragon was angry with the woman, and went off to make war on the rest [remnant in the King James Version] of her children, those who keep the commandments of God and hold the testimony of Jesus."

And Revelation 14:12 reads nearly the same: "Here is a call for the endurance of the saints, those who keep the commandments of God and hold fast to the faith of Jesus."

There they are—two unmistakable characteristics of God's end-time community of faith—#1, they keep the commandments of God, and #2, they have the testimony and faith of Jesus.

Question: Speaking of God's commandments, which one of them is the greatest?

Answer: Listen to "the testimony of Jesus" Himself:

> A lawyer asked [Jesus] a question to test him. "Teacher, which commandment in the law is the greatest?" He said to him, " 'You shall love the Lord your God with all your heart, and with all your soul, and with all your mind.' This is the greatest and first commandment. And a second is like it: 'You shall love your neighbor as yourself.' On these two commandments hang all the law and the prophets."[5]

There it is, the testimony of Jesus Christ Himself. Any end-time community that considers its mission to be the keeping of the commandments of God will be known as a community that loves God supremely and loves its neighbors impartially.

Question: What is the "testimony of Jesus"?

Answer: " 'I give you a new commandment, that you love one another. Just as I have loved you, you also should love one another. By this everyone will know that you are my disciples, if you have love for one another.' "[6]

There it is again, the testimony of Jesus Christ Himself. I repeat, any end-time community that considers its mission to be the possession of the testimony of Jesus will be known as a community that loves one another as Christ has loved them.

You see, it is inescapable even in the Apocalypse. God's end-time community of faith will be a radical demonstration of love for all humanity, sinners and saints alike!

Any church that chooses to be a *museum* for truth instead of a hospital for sinners will rapidly decompose and deteriorate from being a *museum* to becoming a *mausoleum*. Because museums for truth are essentially mausoleums for the dead, not the living! As Jesus bluntly put it: " 'You are like white-washed tombs, which on the outside look beautiful, but inside they are full of the bones of the dead and of all kinds of filth.' "[7]

Losing the vision

Sad, isn't it—when a church loses its vision and mission to be a hospital for sinners?

Listen for a moment to Jim Cymbala, pastor of the 6,000-member Brooklyn Tabernacle in New York City, in his stirring book, *Fresh Wind, Fresh Fire* :

> Christians often hesitate to reach out to those who are different. They want God to clean the fish before they catch them. If someone's gold ring is attached to an unusual body part [had he been writing to Adventists, I suppose he would have chosen to write, "attached to *any* body part"], if the person doesn't smell the best, or if the skin color is not the same, Christians tend to hesitate. But think for a moment about *God* reaching out to *us*. If ever there was a "reach," that was it: the holy, pure Deity extending himself to us who were soiled, evil-hearted, unholy. God could have said, "You're so different from me, so distasteful, I would really rather not get too close to you." But he didn't say that. It was our very differentness that drew his hand of love.
>
> Jesus didn't just speak the healing word to lepers from a distance of thirty yards. He *touched* them.[8]

This is the church God has called us to be.

Society may have to take a stance legally and morally, but never should the church close its doors to those society cannot accept. There is no Megan's Law in the church. You may recall the tragic death of little Megan at the hands of a repeat child abuse offender. New Jersey subsequently passed a law requiring public notification wherever a convicted sex offender should move, irrespective of his having paid his penalty to society in prison. I'm not arguing for the church abandoning its responsibility to protect its innocent young through careful background checks of all whom we enlist to minister to children. But there is no Megan's Law with divine love. No unpardonable, unforgettable sin that bars the sinner—any sinner—either from heaven's ER Physician (Jesus) or from heaven's ER (the church).

"I have come to call sinners to repentance." That is our healing mission too.

Soft on sin or big on sinners?

Are you suggesting that we become *soft* on sin? Not at all. But like Jesus we should become *big* on sinners. You see, there is a world of difference between *condemning* and *condoning*. Many people think that the opposite of condemning is condoning. And so to avoid condemning, they condone. To prove they love the sinner, they erroneously conclude they must affirm the sinner's lifestyle.

Wrong! Jesus did not condemn, but neither did He condone! "You've had five husbands, and the one you're sleeping with now isn't your own!" was His uncompromising stance with the woman at the well.[9] "Neither do I condemn you, but go and sin no more" was His quiet pronouncement to the woman taken in adultery.[10] "Simon, let me tell you a story," was His deft thrust into the heart of the guilty Pharisee he refused to expose in public.[11] Jesus was never soft on sin, but He was always big on the sinner.

Of course it's messy!

The church of Christ must be the same! Of course it's messy being a hospital for sinners, but where else is a messed-up world supposed to turn, if it can't turn to the church of Christ?

"By this will all the world know you are My people, if you have love for one another" means, "By this will all the world know that you are My end-time community of faith, if you become My end-time community of love."

A hospital for sinners—because there can be no more radical love and no more exalted calling for the church than to be like Jesus and become a hospital for sinners.

" 'It is not the healthy who need a doctor, but the sick. I have not come to call the righteous, but sinners.' "[12] A hospital for sinners—that's why Jesus came.

Therefore, I propose that we hang a Red Cross banner from our steeples for all the world to see. I'd like to also propose that we all wear Red Cross armbands where we live and where we study and where we work and where we play. Wouldn't that be something? Everywhere you and I went, the world would see a Red Cross. And they would know the moment they saw it that they could come to you and me for the healing that only the Red Cross can provide.

Because it is no accident that it is red, and it is no mistake that it is a cross. For it was on Calvary's red cross that the Savior of the world expired. It was at that crimson stake that the doors to God's ER and heaven's hospital were thrown wide to an entire race of sinners. "With his stripes, we are healed."[13]

And what does that make us who follow the Christ of Calvary? We are the Church of the Red Cross. And because there is no sin and no sinner not covered by the Red Cross, we are truly an ER hospital *for all.* Which, by the way, is a universal coverage not even Blue Cross can match!

1. Luke 5:27-30.
2. Luke 5:31, 32.
3. Luke 15:1, 2.
4. Luke 7:33, 34, emphasis supplied.
5. Matthew 22:35-40.
6. John 13:34, 35.
7. Matthew 23:27.
8. Jim Cymbala, *Fresh Wind, Fresh Fire,* p. 141, emphasis his.
9. See John 4.
10. See John 8.
11. See Luke 7.
12. Mark 2:17, NIV.
13. Isaiah 53:5, KJV.

I *give you*
a new commandment,
that you love one another.
Just as I have loved you,
you also should love
one another.' "

JOHN 13:34

CHAPTER

7

GLUING
THE GOBLET
BACK TOGETHER

There are three reasons why I wish this page could become a video screen for you right now. Reason #1: I'd like to share with you an experiment we conducted on global satellite a few months ago. Reason #2: It's a whole lot safer to conduct the experiment on video, rather than reenact it live. Reason #3: Though the dramatic point of the experiment remains the same, the conclusions drawn from it have radically shifted from when I first did it on video.

Shattering the goblet

Before we reenact the experiment here on paper, a brief background is in order. In the fall of 1998, I had the privilege of participating in a rather historic global satellite event, the NeXt Millennium Seminar. For five weeks this live seminar was transmitted from the campus congregation I pastor to over a hundred nations in forty languages simultaneously. We called it Net

'98. On night twenty-one, the title of our Bible lecture was, "The Truth of the Broken Goblet." (If you participated in that seminar or have seen the video series, perhaps you'll remember that evening.) In this lecture I imagined that we had the great moral leaders of our world assembled before us in a jury box— well-known religious leaders such as James Dobson and Billy Graham and Pope John Paul II and the Dhali Lama, to name a few. And the lecture essentially became an impassioned appeal to our moral leaders to call their followers back to the moral law of God.

The whole point of the lecture and the experiment we conducted was based on the stunning declaration in a short New Testament epistle called James: "For whoever keeps the whole law and yet stumbles at just one point is guilty of breaking all of it. For he who said, 'Do not commit adultery,' also said, 'Do not murder.' If you do not commit adultery but do commit murder, you have become a law-breaker."[1]

It was to illustrate James's dramatic declaration—that when you break one of the commandments of God's great moral law, you essentially break the entire law—that we conducted an experiment on satellite camera to prove it. The reason I'm glad we're not doing it live together right now is because I somehow got the laws of physics a bit mixed up that night.

Before the program I met with our director on stage to rehearse the experiment. It was to be a simple experiment where a glass goblet would be placed before the audience, after which I would take a hammer and shatter it while everyone watched there in the Pioneer Memorial Church and around the world via satellite.

Our director Bruce was worried that the shattered glass might fly out over the audience. But I assured him that having conducted this experiment once before, the glass actually flew backwards instead.

"Are you sure?" he pressed me.

"Yes, I'm sure."

Well, just to be safe, Bruce taped the base of the glass goblet to a stand, so at least the neck itself of the goblet wouldn't fly away. We then draped the goblet and stand and left it there on the platform beside me until the appropriate moment.

The moment came soon enough. And with the cameras rolling, I stepped away from the lectern, picked up a hammer, removed the drape and proceeded to half vigorously, half gingerly strike the glass goblet. And sure enough the glass shattered.

But alas, the laws of physics abandoned me that night! Bruce proved right, for when I shattered the goblet, pieces of glass shot out over the front row of the audience, where our co-hosts Bernie and Shasta were sitting. And while I gamely plowed on with my lecture, I saw out of the corner of my eye our floor director actually on the floor on all fours, frantically trying to pick up all the shards of the broken goblet and stay out of the cameras' line of sight. It really was "the truth of the broken goblet" all over the place!

Some weeks later when I was talking with my congregation about that memorable back-firing moment, one of our university physicists later emailed me with the assurance that the laws of physics hadn't been broken that night. The difference in the direction of the flying glass was caused by taping the base to the stand when the experiment was conducted the second time. By taping the base, Dr. Clark Rowland wrote, "the glass tended to explode in all directions. When the tape was not there, there would have been much greater velocity toward the back of the platform as you earlier observed." Which only goes to prove that whether you're a director or a preacher, you can't change the laws of physics, can you?

That, by the way, was the very point the experiment was making that night on satellite. Because no matter which way the glass shattered, the truth is the same: When you break a portion of a goblet, you shatter the entire goblet. That is James's truth, too: When you break a portion of God's law, you break it all.

For our moral leaders to call the nation back to God and His law—and yet all the while disregard the seventh-day Sabbath of the fourth commandment—is a recipe for continued moral decline and failure. How did James put it? "For whoever keeps the whole law and yet stumbles at just one point is guilty of breaking all of it."[2]

James's radical point

But why go back and make that point all over again right here? Let me be candid with you. A careful re-reading and re-examination of James 2 make it painfully clear that our application on that satellite evening fell short of the radical point James is actually making. Oh yes, Seventh-day Adventists do well to draw the attention of their Christian friends and neighbors to James's stunning point that you cannot break one of the Ten Commandments—take the fourth commandment for example, "Remember the seventh-day Sabbath to keep it holy"—without in turn shattering the entire Decalogue. That conclusion rightfully and powerfully can be made from James 2:10. So we need make no apology at all for what we shared with the world that night in November.

However, as it turns out, to make his point, James is *not* championing the *fourth* commandment. Instead he is passionately appealing for the *eleventh* commandment! For generations we've turned to James 2 for the fourth commandment, when in fact it is a powerful defense of the eleventh commandment!

Let's go back and rediscover the James 2 truth we've missed for all these years:

> My brothers and sisters, do you with your acts of favoritism really believe in our glorious Lord Jesus Christ? For if a person with gold rings and in fine clothes comes into your assembly, and if a poor person in dirty clothes also comes in, and if you take notice of the one wearing the fine clothes and say, "Have a seat here, please," while to one who is poor you say, "Stand here," or, "Sit at my feet," have you not made distinctions [discriminated, NIV] among yourselves, and become judges with evil thoughts?[3]

The day versus the way

James is writing to Christians like you and me who already are worshiping on the seventh-day Sabbath. So he's not concerned about the *day* of the Sabbath, but rather the *way* of the Sabbath.

"I don't understand you," he pens. "Here we are—all of us in church on the Sabbath [and the word James uses for "assembly" is actually *synagogen* or "synagogue," making this the only place in the New Testament where "synagogue" is applied to the Christian church]—on this day that celebrates our common Creator and Father and God. And there you are treating some of God's children with rank favoritism and partiality and discrimination, when you know that we, poor and rich alike, are all children of the same heavenly Father. What's the matter with you? Why are you engaged in such blatant favoritism and partiality for the rich? It's just plain wrong!"

To underscore his point, James launches an unsubtle critique of the wealthy:

> Listen, my beloved brothers and sisters. Has not God chosen the poor in the world to be rich in faith and to be heirs of the kingdom that he has promised to those who love him? But you have dishonored the poor. Is it not the rich who oppress you? Is it not they who drag you into court? Is it not they who blaspheme the excellent name that was invoked over you?[4]

To the wealthy Christian who is reading these words right now, you need to know that James is not describing rich Christians. Rather he is referring to wealthy *non*-Christians. He is dealing with the socio-economic reality of the fledgling Christian church in the Roman Empire. Namely that Christianity back then—as it has over the centuries—predominantly attracted the poor and the marginalized and the alienated and the disenfranchised. The impoverished masses comprised the vast majority of those who were drawn to the liberating truth from Jesus and about Jesus. By and large, it was the poor, not the rich, who were joining the church.

Which is precisely James's point. "Most of you are poor— you were born that way and you'll die that way—so why all your foolish partiality and favoritism to the wealthy who show up in your churches now and then? Don't you understand these are the very ones who've been oppressing you? Come on, people! From a strictly human point of view, what silliness leads you who are already poor to kow-tow to your rich visitors and discriminate against your poor visitors, whose economic plight you know rather intimately by first-hand experience?"

By the way, James isn't finished with his exposé of the wealthy of the empire! Before his letter ends, he'll return to his condemnation of economic disparity:

> Come now, you rich people, weep and wail for the miseries that are coming to you. Your riches have rotted, and your clothes are moth-eaten. Your gold and silver have rusted, and their rust will be evidence against you, and it will eat your flesh like fire. You have laid up treasure for the last days. Listen! The wages of the laborers who mowed your fields, which you kept back by fraud, cry out, and the cries of the harvesters have reached the ears of the Lord of hosts. You have lived on the earth in luxury and in pleasure; you have fattened your hearts in a day of slaughter. You have condemned and murdered the righteous one, who does not resist you.[5]

"Have's" and "have-not's"

What is so troubling in this new millennium is that economic disparity and injustice still stalk our nation and our world. The sins James cries out against are still ours. What happened at the end of the last century and millennium in Seattle may indeed be a warning shot across society's bow! We all remember the television images of those rioters who trashed the downtown business district in protest over the World Trade Organization. Labor unions, environmentalists, and ecological activists joined together in protesting an organization they believe is fueled by multinational conglomerates that are exploiting the masses and labor forces of East and West—all for the sake of greed and profit.

Whether their belief was valid or not is not the point. And who started the rioting and looting is immaterial. The point is that James warns wealthy nations and wealthy corporations and wealthy investors and wealthy executives and wealthy employers (Adventists, other Christians, or otherwise), who have exploited the poor laborer to reap their profits: "You will pay dearly when in the last days the bloody cry of the laborer will rise up in violent protest!"

James's ominous prediction clearly portends the coming day when the criminal divide between the "have's" and the "have-not's" will explode into global chaos and social carnage. "You have lived on the earth in luxury and in pleasure; you have fattened your hearts in a day of slaughter."[6]

There was a time when labor unions were thought to be dead and gone, their political clout eroded, their ability to organize and rally disenchanted workers and laborers dissipated. But a resurging labor movement is now vowing to fight the economic powerhouses of the world. It may indeed be a harbinger of dark days yet to come. For a century ago this sentence was written: "The trade unions will be one of the agencies that will bring upon this earth a time of trouble such as has not been since the world began."[7] And it will be precipitated by the criminal neglect of the poor by the rich—or as Jesus' parable cast it, the hellish chasm between the rich man and poor Lazarus.

"That's why I don't understand you," James writes. "Why do you discriminate against the poor when you are the oppressed poor, yourselves?"

The fact is—even as it was back then, it is so today—the wealthy by and large, have never been attracted to the radical self-sacrifice of Christ and the Cross and Christianity. Because the more wealth you accumulate, the more preoccupied you will become with that wealth, and the more likely you will worship your own ability to gain that wealth. Which is why Jesus one day remarked to His disciples, "It is easier for a camel to go through the eye of a needle [try pulling that off sometime!] than for someone who is rich to enter into the kingdom of God."

And the disciples exclaimed, "Wow! Who then can be saved!"

To which Jesus replied, "Ah, but what may look impossible to man, is possible with God!"[8] Because God can save even the wealthy, if they desire. There can be only one God, and if they will choose Him over their riches (we have the word of Jesus on it), God will save the wealthy!

For that reason it is vital that you who are wealthy followers of Christ develop personal friendships within your professional relationships with your wealthy colleagues and influential peers. The poor cannot reach the rich, but you can. Jesus promised that what a camel and a needle couldn't do, God can do—He can save the rich. So share your Jesus with those who respect you as a peer, who will listen to you as they will to no other friend of God's.

The royal law

But James isn't quite through yet, and so he hurries on to his punch line: "You do well if you really fulfill the royal law according to the scripture, 'You shall love your neighbor as yourself.' "[9] And what is this "royal law" of which he writes? It obviously is the supreme law and commandment of the King. And what did the King command us the night before His execution? " 'I give you a new commandment, that you love one another. Just as I have loved you, you also should love one another. By this everyone will know that you are my disciples, if you have love for one another.' "[10] The royal law is the eleventh commandment, the commandment of the King.

And so wealthy, poor, or middle class—what does it matter? James writes. You are to love them all as the King commanded!

And then comes his zinger: "But if you show partiality, you commit sin and are convicted by the law as transgressors. For whoever keeps the whole law but fails in one point has become accountable for all of it."[11]

Mark it well. The one law James cites, whose violation will shatter the entire Ten Commandments, is the royal law. He doesn't cite the fourth commandment, as critical as that is. He cites the eleventh commandment. "You shall love your neighbor as yourself." Or as Jesus expressed it that fateful Thursday night, "Love one another as I have loved you." Without distinction or discrimination, without favoritism or partiality. Love your neighbor, love one another, love every single one.

Choosing *not* to love

And, if we're willing to be brutally honest with ourselves, this is exactly where the painful rub is. Oh sure, we are all very proficient at loving the lovely and adoring the lovable. But *PLEASE* , dear God, do not ask me to love the *un*-lovely or the *un*-lovable!

I'm going to let Douglas Cooper in his book, *Living God's Love*, remind us all of the kinds of people we have chosen *not* to love:

> Tolerating someone who may irritate us, or who may be unappealing to us is one thing. After all, *they* have *problems*, we reason. We must try to tolerate their deficiencies. But as for becoming actually involved *with* them *in*

their problems in a loving, caring way and assisting them toward wholeness, mentally, physically, or spiritually— well, this is something else. This demands something more. A great deal more. It is seldom done.

We tend rather to restrict our interest to only the "fun" people, the attractive people. Those who smell nice, who exhibit pleasant behavior, speech . . . —those who dress well, who keep their hair carefully combed and their teeth brushed.

We covet their company. We like to ask them to an after-church dinner. These are "our" type of people. We have much in common with them. They think like we do. They appeal to us.

That leaves the old, the ugly, the boring, the embarrassing, the intellectually inferior. That leaves those we judge immoral or otherwise undesirable. These we leave alone at church services or social functions.

Oh, we manage the token gestures. The recognition of their existence. The halfhearted handshake. The guilty, nervous, condescendingly-toned question about their health. The forced interest in what they tell us. But all the while we make it perfectly clear that we expect them to keep their distance and to know their place. The pet at home fares as well or better.

Some we even feel justified in rejecting. Like the hostile. Or the critical. Those who seem always to cause tension and frustration because of their eternal negativism. Those who seem forever spitting on people with words. Those who are repugnant because they talk too much. Those who make us uncomfortable because they talk too little. The crude. The flippant. The super-egotistical.

To us, these unappealing, unlovely souls we justify ourselves in rejecting.

Can we not only tolerate and accept such people, but also love them and minister to them as well?[12]

Wow! Not only is Cooper comprehensively blunt, but he's also bluntly comprehensive in reminding all of us how easily we dismiss the unlovely and how thoughtlessly we discriminate against the unlovable.

The Christian caste system

It makes me wonder sometimes if our church is any different than India. Could it be that we, too, embrace an unspoken but very unsubtle caste system? "After all, I am *more educated* than you, which is why I can call you and write you by your first name, but I expect you to address me by my title." Living in a university community, it is only too clear that some Christians mistake academic achievement for personal or social superiority; and that's sad. Whenever a person has to insist that his title be spoken whenever his name is called, the issue really isn't superiority, but insecurity, isn't it?

"After all, I am *wealthier* than you." But since when has personal wealth been an accurate barometer of personal worth? The compelling precedent of God incarnating Himself in a dirt-poor family for His human sojourn here ought to be evidence enough that financial accumulation is a bankrupted measuring stick for either moral value or eternal rank.

"After all, I am *more placed* than you." More what? "Well, you know—more highly positioned and placed in the hierarchy of the church than you are." Just like the Pharisees, right? Who stood on the street corners and intoned and prayed in such stain-glassed voices that those who didn't know any better were fooled into believing that the position made the person. But how sad to live by that caste system! Because as the parable of Christ painfully exposed, it was the tax collector who went home from church that Sabbath declared right with God—not the placed and positioned Pharisee.[13]

How do we really treat those who are different from us? Not just in terms of personal achievement or accomplishment, but what about our differences of opinion? I've heard of congregations who have literally split in half over differences of worship preference! Like the old adage quips, "You worship God in your way, and I'll worship Him in *His*." Because we're all pretty much convinced that *our* way is indeed *His* way. And that's sad too. Just as sad as discriminating between the rich and the poor, is accepting or rejecting one another on the basis of our worship preferences. Does the body of Christ have to be torn apart in order to prove your personal point? And if it does, then are you suggesting that if my tastes are different from yours, I don't belong? How many people are you willing to shut the door to in order to preserve your own personal preference and opinion? It makes one wonder—have we made a god out of personal preference? How sad!

And what about our subtle caste system of theological differences? Are we supposed to love people who differ from us theologically or are we called by God to destroy them at any cost? Do we really believe that the Spirit of Jesus compels us to raise thousands of dollars in order to publish our attacks and promote our criticisms? Is that what Jesus meant when He gave us the eleventh commandment to "love one another"? I've heard of congregations split down the middle, fighting over the human nature of our Lord Jesus. Can you believe it?

Fighting over the humanity of the God-Man who gave us the eleventh commandment. You may win that argument, but you'll lose the battle every time. And that's sad, very sad.

And the list goes on and on. Because that's what happens when you live by the enslaving codes of a caste system. The enemy of unity has devised an interminable catalog of ways and walls to devilishly divide us. "Let them go somewhere else; we don't need 'em around here!"

"Oh, but we do," both James and Jesus cry out. The royal law and the eleventh commandment are utterly clear: God has no favorites, and neither can His church.

God's favorite child

When I think of my own sin of partiality and favoritism and my own inability at times to genuinely love the unlovely, I remember the delightful story Brennan Manning recalls in his book, *Lion and Lamb,* the story told by a graduate professor of his, an old Dutchman:

> I'm one of thirteen children. One day when I was playing in the street of our hometown in Holland, I got thirsty and came into the pantry of our house for a glass of water. It was around noon and my father had just come home from work to have lunch. He was sitting at the kitchen table . . . with a neighbor. A door separated the kitchen from the pantry and my father didn't know that I was there. The neighbor said to my father, "Joe, there's something I've wanted to ask you for a long time, but if it's too personal, just forget I ever asked." "What is your question?"
>
> "Well, you have thirteen children. Out of all of them

is there one that is your favorite, one you love more than all the others?"

I had my ear pressed against the door, hoping against hope it would be me. "That's easy," my father said. "Sure there's one I love more than all the others. That's Mary, the twelve-year-old. She just got braces on her teeth and feels so awkward and embarrassed that she won't go out of the house anymore. Oh, but you asked about my favorite. That's my twenty-three-year-old Peter. His fiancée just broke their engagement, and he is desolate. But the one I really love the most is little Michael. He's totally uncoordinated and terrible in any sport he tries to play. The other kids on the street make fun of him. But, of course, the apple of my eye is Susan. Only twenty-four, living in her own apartment, and developing a drinking problem. I cry for Susan. But I guess of all the kids . . ." and my father went on mentioning each of his thirteen children by name.[14]

"Red and yellow, black and white, all are precious in His sight." So tell us, God, which one of us is Your favorite? And one by one, He tells us, as He goes down the list of His six billion children on earth. That is precisely why James is unequivocal in declaring partiality to be sin. Partiality is a sin simply because it is so contrary to the life and love of God, who has no favorites, but who truly, deeply, eternally loves us all!

I got a note from a parishioner who remembered a Sabbath when she was feeling so low and discouraged, and apparently somewhere during the sermon the preacher looked in her direction and declared, "You are God's beloved." The very thought, she wrote, swept her despondent spirits heavenward. To this day she can't remember the rest of the sermon, but she went home aglow that Sabbath with the thought that she was beloved of God.

That's the way it is with the truth of Calvary—the truth about the Father who gave His Son to win back the hearts of this rebel race. It is truly such glorious news, that we can go home every Sabbath of the year and every day of the week with the realization that the Father of Jesus loves us dearly.

And that is why His royal law commands us to do the same for every single one of His beloved children: "A new commandment I give you that you love one another. By this the whole world will know you are My people, if you have love for one another."

You see, we thought it was disregard of the fourth commandment that broke the crystal goblet—and for some it is. But it turns out for those of us who have "mastered" the Ten, it is disobedience to the eleventh commandment that breaks the crystal goblet of God's royal law.

I know we're right about the *day* of the royal law. But upon the dawning of a new millennium, surely the time has come for us to be right about the *way* of the royal law too. For have not Jesus and James admonished us to love every single one?

Amen.

Edna Bow Cheney, a social worker in Boston, Massachusetts, wrote a beautiful prayer a century ago:

At first I prayed for light: Could I but see the way,
How gladly, swiftly would I walk to everlasting day.
And next I prayed for strength: That I might tread the road
With firm, unfaltering feet, and win the heaven's serene abode.
And then I asked for faith: Could I but trust my God,
I'd live enfolded in His peace, though foes were all abroad.

But now I pray for love: Deep love to God and man,
A living love that will not fail, however dark His plan.
And light and strength and faith are opening everywhere!
God waited patiently until I prayed the larger prayer.[15]

   Amen.

---

1. James 2:10, 11, NIV.
2. James 2:10.
3. James 2:1-4.
4. James 2:5-7.
5. James 5:1-6.
6. James 5:5.
7. Ellen White, Letter 200, 1903 (*Country Living,* p.10).
8. See Matthew 19:24-26.
9. James 2:8.
10. John 13:34, 35.
11. James 2:9, 10.
12. Douglas Cooper, *Living God's Love,* pp. 41, 42.
13. See Luke 18:9-14.
14. Brennan Manning, *Lion and Lamb,* pp. 22, 23.
15. *Seventh-day Adventist Hymnal,* No. 488.

I *give you*
a new commandment,
that you love one another.
Just as I have loved you,
you also should love
one another.' "

JOHN 13:34

CHAPTER 8

THE GOOD SAM CLUB

Can you take the eleventh commandment too far? Is there a sensible limit in loving your neighbor?

Let me be more specific. Would you bring a homeless, convicted sex offender into your own home to live—in order to obey the command of God to love your neighbor as yourself? Would you still do it, if you had two small children?

No storybook ending

The story you're about to read is true. The Associated Press reported it with a headline that would catch anybody's eye: "Couple test faith by taking in sex offender—Neighborhood angry about ex-con moving in with family of four." The provocative story was datelined Danville, Kentucky. AP writer Allen Breed began it with these words: "It's a story of a neighborhood losing its innocence, of a couple testing their faith, of an ex-con seeking a second chance. But it doesn't have a storybook ending."[1]

But let's hit the pause button for moment. It's precisely because it doesn't have a "storybook ending" that this story seems the right story to read straight into the narrative of that sunny afternoon when a city-slicker lawyer stood up, cleared his throat, and set out to embarrass an itinerant country preacher in front of the whole crowd. Oh sure, we could read the classic story Jesus told in response to that lawyerly grilling. But not this time. The Good Samaritan can be saved for another occasion.[2] Instead, this time let's read into the record the story of the sex-offender the Kentucky couple brought home to live.

Because I fear that the well-worn, universally beloved, overly-familiar parable of the good Samaritan—a story we have heard and read and rushed through so many times now—I'm afraid we're nearly impervious these days to its radical and revolutionary punch line. It simply doesn't move us anymore. Because, let's face it, nobody's in the mood for revolution any more, except perhaps for a few aging Boomer hippies who now tuck their ponytails inside their Stetson hats.

Besides, why would anybody want to live that radically any more, when the biggest thrill society can muster these days is riding the congested sidewalks of New York on a collapsible silver Razor push scooter, or an afternoon of high-adrenalin, online day trading on the Nasdaq with a cup of Starbucks cappuccino for support. The world has neither the stomach nor the time for anything more "rad."

Hence, it does seem a bit corny even talking about some foreigner called a Samaritan stopping on a mountain road to help a motorist in distress, when you can turn on the TV and have Arnold Schwartzeneggar terminating every living thing in sight. Which is why substituting the story of sex-offender Nate Sims and the compassionate LaPalmes family may make the point stick with this next-millennium generation just about as well as any story.

So back to the story.

Luke 10 actually sets up the Danville, Kentucky story for us, so let's at least read its preamble:

> Just then a lawyer stood up to test Jesus. "Teacher," he said, "what must I do to inherit eternal life?" He said to him, "What is written in the law? What do you read there?" He answered, "You shall love the Lord your God with all your heart, and with all your soul, and with all your strength, and with all your mind; and your neighbor as yourself." And he said to him, "You have given the right answer; do this, and you will live."
>
> But wanting to justify himself, he asked Jesus, "And who is my neighbor?"[3]

Who is my neighbor?

Is a convicted sex-offender my neighbor? Is a homeless White man who rummages through my garbage my neighbor? Is a Black man who doesn't live in my neighborhood my neighbor? Is a young man suffering with AIDS my neighbor? Is an elderly woman dying of cancer my neighbor? Is an inner-city baby my neighbor? How about the baby's unwed mother?

Is the chief of police my neighbor? Are *any* police my neighbor? Is a socially-retarded and behaviorally-odd student on campus my neighbor? Is a mentally-retarded woman my neighbor?

Is a Roman Catholic my neighbor? How about a Baptist? A Mormon? A Jehovah's Witness? A Jew? A Hindu? A Moslem?

Is an unemployed drug addict my neighbor? How about an employed alcoholic?

Is my next-door neighbor my neighbor any more? How about the ones across the street—do they count?

"But who is my neighbor?" the lawyer wanted to know.

And Jesus wanted him to know. So He told the story of the good Samaritan. Instead, let's listen to this very contemporary story with its own version of "good" and "Samaritan" and its own compelling answer to the lawyer's question, "Who is my neighbor?"

The story of the Christian couple and the sex offender

It's a story of a neighborhood losing its innocence, of a couple testing their faith, of an ex-con seeking a second chance. But it doesn't have a storybook ending.

After 20 years in prison, Nate Sims returned in late July to Danville, the quaint college town where he had settled as a teen-ager. Within days, his picture was in the local newspaper; next to it were the phrases "sex offender" and "high risk." He had been convicted of rape and sodomy.

He immediately lost his new job at a packaging plant and was soon living out of his rattletrap car. Under Kentucky's newly-enacted Megan's Law, named for a 7-year-old New Jersey girl murdered by a released molester living in her neighborhood, Sims was arrested for not being at the address he'd reported to parole officials.

Then suddenly everything changed.

One day on television, Tammy LaPalme saw a tall man running from a camera crew. She recognized him from a newspaper article headllined: "Boyle (County) registers first high risk sex offender."

"It felt like a sign from God," Mark LaPalme said.

He and his wife asked themselves the question printed on a pink and yellow cloth bracelet that she wears: "What Would Jesus Do?"

Mark and Tammy LaPalme explained that they were "baby Christians," out to test their newfound, born-again faith. [So] they decided to open their five-bedroom home to someone needing shelter.

"I mean, we felt like God's blessed us in so many ways," said Mark LaPalme, 38, a gangly man with an earnest voice. "We've been so selfish with it up to now."

[And so] instead of a jail cell, the 52-year-old Sims found himself living in a $150,000 house in upscale Riverview Estates—with a couple who trusted him enough to bed him down across the hall from their children's play-room.

"I was in shock," Sims said recently in a voice that seemed too soft to have come from his 6-foot-4 frame. "I ain't never had anyone lift a hand for me."

Sims moved in on Aug. 12. "I told Mark and Tammy, 'I hope you all know what you're getting into,' " Sims recalled last week as he sat at their dining room table.

Everything happened so fast that the LaPalmes never

bothered to inform their neighbors. They didn't have to.

Bright yellow fliers soon appeared everywhere in Riverview—in newspaper boxes, on street lights, even stapled to the leaves of bushes.

"!!BEWARE!! Sex Offender at Mark and Tammy LaPalme's residence," they said, giving the address and the phone number.

Letters started coming. An anonymous writer complained: "You say to 'Love thy neighbor,' but you are demonstrating a total disregard for our feelings, our fears, and our safety. That's not my idea of a good 'neighbor.' "

Streets normally filled with twilight walkers and kids on bicycles were suddenly desolate. People who never locked their doors started shuttering up at night and looking into alarm systems.

The LaPalmes responded by pulling down the notification leaflets and replacing them with white fliers of their own. "Let he who is without sin cast the first stone!" the sheets said, quoting Bible verses on forgiveness and brotherly love.

Attorney Bruce Petrie, a neighbor who describes himself as born again, was not swayed: "My understanding of my Christian duty is first to my family."

Neighbor Jill Lee's college-age daughter began calling on a cell phone to be escorted from her car to the house and her 8-year-old son was placed under virtual house arrest.

Neighborhood kids stopped visiting the LaPalmes' children—daughter Sydney, 8, and son Tyler, 7. One neighbor came by LaPalme's car lot in nearby Harrodsburg to complain that he'd ruined his chances of selling his home.

"You moved a nuclear waste dump right next to me," he told LaPalme. . . .

Neighbors couldn't believe that the LaPalmes would expose their children to such risks. Mark LaPalme said the family was not fearful. . . .

Then, as suddenly as he had arrived, Sims left the neighborhood.

Returning to the LaPalme's house Monday after his first day at a new job cleaning uniforms, he found a camera crew from the syndicated television show "Extra" waiting for him. He packed his bags and fled without even saying goodbye.[4]

How much love is enough?

How far should we go in loving our neighbor?

Did this family of (as they called themselves) "baby Christians" go too far? What about the words on the wife's pink and yellow bracelet—"What Would Jesus Do?" Is this what Jesus would do? Would you offer your home as a refuge to a convicted sex offender?

What if I told you the LaPalmes family was Black and Nate Sims was White? What if I told you Nate Sims, the ex-con, was Black and the LaPalmes were White? I'm not going to tell you. Although Jesus certainly didn't spare the racial details in that headline story He borrowed out of the daily news! He didn't mind telling who was who—a Jewish victim, a Jewish clergyman, a Jewish elder, and a Samaritan businessman. As we noted, it took *chutzpah* to even mention a Samaritan, but it took sheer daring to make the Samaritan the hero of the story before that Jewish audience! But then Jesus was never afraid of publicly lancing the social sores and racial sins of His day, now was He?

And when He gets to the end of that news story, Jesus turns to the lawyer and asks the inescapable question: Which one of the neighbors in Danville was the genuine neighbor to Nate Sims? Attorney Bruce Petrie, who describes himself as a born again Christian, but who refused to help the ex-sex-offender? Neighbor Jill Lee who wouldn't let her children play with the LaPalme children? Mark and Tammy LaPalme who took in the homeless former sex-offender?

"Which one in Danville, Mr. Lawyer, was neighbor to Nate Sims?" And when the lawyer wouldn't even mention the name, but instead mumbled, "The ones who showed him mercy," Jesus was ready with His radical and revolutionary punch line: "Go and do likewise' "![5]

Do what?

Show mercy.

To whom?

Your neighbor.

And who is my neighbor?

Both the good Samaritan and the Danville stories make it incontrovertibly clear—our neighbor, your neighbor, my neighbor is *anyone who is in need.*

But would that include a convicted sex-offender? How about a homeless White man who rummages through my garbage? Is a Black man who doesn't live in my neighborhood my neighbor? Is a young man suffering with AIDS my neighbor? Is an elderly woman dying of cancer my neighbor? Is an inner-city baby my neighbor? How about the baby's unwed mother?

Is a socially-retarded and behaviorally-odd student on campus my neighbor? Is a mentally-retarded woman my neighbor? Is an unemployed drug addict my neighbor? How about an employed alcoholic?

Is my next-door neighbor my neighbor any more? How about the ones across the street—do they count?

Showing mercy to those in need

Listen to this classic summation of Jesus' punch line to the parable of the good Samaritan in *The Desire of Ages*:

> Thus the question, "Who is my neighbor?" is forever answered. Christ has shown that our neighbor does not mean merely one of the church or faith to which we belong. It has no reference to race, color, or class distinction. Our neighbor is every person who needs our help. Our neighbor is every soul who is wounded and bruised by the adversary. Our neighbor is everyone who is the property of God.[6]

Did you catch those three categories? Our neighbor is: #1, every person who needs our help; #2, every soul who is wounded and bruised by the adversary; and, #3, everyone who is the property of God. Plain and simple—*every last human being!*

And so "baby Christian" Tammy LaPalme is minding her own business, watching TV one day, when she spots on the local news a man running away from a television crew and recognizes the face from a newspaper article announcing the return of a former sex offender to Danville. And her heart is touched—not only to feel sorry for the plight of this apparently still-unforgiven man—

but she is moved to do something concrete about his desperate need.

And what did she do?

She showed mercy. She and her husband Mark simply reached out and offered that ex-con what he needed most of all at that moment—the security of human compassion and the safety of Christian love. Down to the jail they went with their offer: "You can live with us." And he did—until the un-neighborly neighbors drove him out.

"And who is my neighbor?"

My neighbor is anyone who is in need.

And what shall I do with my neighbor?

Love her.

How shall I love my neighbor?

Show him mercy.

The "Good Sam Club"

Join the Good Sam Club, and show mercy. Because God knows that woman doesn't *deserve* mercy. (Mercy deserved is actually pity.) And you know that if the tables were turned, that man wouldn't give you a drop of mercy. But as it so happens today— she's the one wounded and broken, a wreck by the side of the road. He's the one this time utterly helpless, abandoned by the rest of his world—his family, his friends, his colleagues—left alone without defense.

Oh sure, you can walk by and pretend you don't know or pretend you didn't see or pretend you don't care. But you also know down deep in your own soul that the very sight of him, the very thought of her, awakens a pang of conscience and a stab of compassion.

My friend, act on your conscience; act out your compassion.

Listen to your heart that whispers, "It is time for me to show mercy."

It may mean burying the hatchet with an enemy or it may mean lending a hand to a stranger. It could mean offering a cup of water or it may mean giving a donation of cash. It could be sharing your holiday dinner or it may mean volunteering your vacation time.

I know of one family that at Christmas forgoes the ritual of giving gifts to each other and, instead, adopts a family in need and gives their gifts to them. The point is, it doesn't take a Ph.D. in neighborliness to show mercy and to love your neighbor as yourself.

I know students on my campus who have volunteered to tutor inner-city children in nearby Benton Harbor twice a week for two hours each time. The point is, it doesn't take a Ph.D. in neighborliness to show mercy and to love your neighbor as yourself.

I know a gentleman who goes from grocery store to grocery store every week, picking up discarded produce and day-old bakery goods and damaged, un-sellable food cans and cartons—and then drives through the student housing of our university, serving those in need out of his open trunk. The point is, it doesn't take a Ph.D. in neighborliness to show mercy and to love your neighbor as yourself.

All it takes is the heart of the good Samaritan.

And where do you get that heart?

You get it from Jesus, the very Good Samaritan, that's where.

And how do you get it from Him?

You ask for it.

Do what a friend of mine does—begin every day with this quiet prayer: "Lord, lead me today to someone to whom I can speak a word of kindness or lend a hand of assistance or offer an embrace of compassion. Lead me to someone today who needs a good neighbor. I don't need to save the world today, just let me make a small difference this day in one life, I pray. Amen."

It's the prayer of the Good Samaritan, is it not? The Good Samaritan who hurried across the galactic chasms to this God-forsaken stretch of midnight where you and I lay, battered and wounded and dying—sex offenders and sin offenders and repeat offenders, all of us. The Good Samaritan who was born in a box of feed and died on a cross of shame—all because Love came to kneel in the dirt beside us, to bind our wounds and heal our lives and save our souls.

It is the prayer of the Good Samaritan. A simple prayer that is proof you cannot take the eleventh commandment too far, for who can take it further than Jesus? " 'I give you a new commandment, that you love one another. Just as I have loved you, you also should love one another.' "[7]

It is a quiet prayer that at this dawning of a new millennium not only seems the right prayer to pray . . . it seems the right prayer to live:

> Lord, make me an instrument of Your peace.
> Where there is hatred, let me sow love.
> Where there is injury, pardon.
> Where there is doubt, faith.
> Where there is despair, hope.
> Where there is darkness, light.
> Where there is sadness, joy.
> O divine Master, grant that I may not so much seek
>   to be   consoled as to console.

To be understood as to understand.
To be loved as to love.
For it is in giving that we receive.
It is in pardoning that we are pardoned.
It is in dying that we are born to eternal life.[8]

---

1 *South Bend Tribune,* September 2, 1999.
2 Luke 10:25-37.
3 Luke 10:25-29.
4 *South Bend Tribune,* September 2, 1999.
5 Luke 10:37.
6 *The Desire of Ages,* p. 503.
7 John 13:34.
8 The prayer of Francis of Assisi.

I *give you*
a new commandment,
that you love one another.
Just as I have loved you,
you also should love
one another.' "

JOHN 13:34

A WORD AFTER

The Reuben Donnelly Company of Chicago is one of the world's largest printers of magazines. The company has a machine that prints and mails notices to people whose subscriptions have expired. One day the machine was whirring through its assignments, when a tiny spring inside it snapped. As a result, the machine typed the same subscription notification 9,734 times to one hapless rancher in Powder Bluff, Colorado. Overwhelmed with those 9,734 reminders that his subscription to *National Geographic* magazine was expiring, the poor man drove the ten miles into town and mailed his subscription money to *National Geographic* with the following note: "Send me the magazine. I give up!"[1]

All through this book you and I have visited and revisited the eleventh commandment. Over and over again we have heard God repeat Himself: Love one another, love one another, love one another. Until maybe like the rancher the time has come for us to dash the message back to Him: "Send me that love. I give up!"

Because surely by now it is clear, the love that God commands of us is the love that He first commends to us. He asks only that which He first gives. What could be fairer and more available than a love like that!

"Send me that love. I give up!"

For that reason John, the great apostle of love, offers his summation: "Beloved, let us love one another, because love is from God; everyone who loves is born of God and knows God. . . . In this is love, not that we loved God but that he loved us and sent his Son to be the atoning sacrifice for our sins. . . . We love because he first loved us."[2] In the shadows of the Cross Jesus breathed the eleventh commandment. He asked only that which He first gave. "He first loved us."

"Send me that love. I give up!"

In the words of Simon Tugwell, "So long as we imagine it is we who have to look for God, we must often lose heart. But it is the other way about—He is looking for us."[3] Glad tidings for our faint hearts! We may call off our frantic search for Him. For "He is looking for us." With the Song of Songs we can jubilantly sing, "I am my beloved's, and his desire is for me."[4]

"Send me that love. I give up!"

In my Bible I have carried these words on a scrap of paper for years, an eloquent portrayal of that great fount from whence flows the only love that can yet slake our thirst:

> All the paternal love which has come down from generation to generation through the channel of human hearts, all the springs of tenderness which have opened in the souls of men [and women], are but a tiny rill to the boundless ocean when compared with the infinite, exhaustless love of God. Tongue cannot utter it; pen

cannot portray it. You may meditate upon it every day of your life; you may search the Scriptures diligently in order to understand it; you may summon every power and capability that God has given you, in the endeavor to comprehend the love and compassion of the heavenly Father; and yet there is an infinity beyond. You may study that love for ages; yet you can never fully comprehend the length and breadth, the depth and the height, of the love of God in giving His Son to die for the world. Eternity itself can never fully reveal it.[5]

Not even 9,734 times a million revelations of God's love will suffice. For "eternity itself can never fully reveal it." And yet in the eleventh commandment God quietly asks for you and me to begin revealing it . . . here . . . and now.

Hence, what could be more fitting an Amen than this prayer? "Send me that love. I give up!"

Amen and amen.

---

1. Nancy Beck Irland and Peter Beck, *Out of This World,* p. 148
2. 1 John 4:7, 10, 19.
3. Quoted in *The Sacred Romance,* Brent Curtis and John Eldredge, p. 69.
4. Song of Solomon 7:10.
5. Ellen White, *Testimonies for the Church,* vol. 5, p. 740.

If you enjoyed this book, you'll enjoy these as well:

Outrageous Grace

Dwight Nelson. This dynamic guide to finding a forever friendship with God was used during NET '98. Perfect for sharing with friends and neighbors.
0-8163-1679-1. Paperback.
US$1.99, Cdn$2.99 each.
US$7.50, Cdn$11.49 five-pack

Living God's Love

Douglas Cooper. This best-selling manual on loving is back at last! Cooper's poignant message is ever fresh and demands the attention of a new generation of Christians who dare to love as Jesus loved.
English 0-8163-1260-5. Paperback. US$5.97, Cdn$8.97.
Spanish 1-5755-4069-X. Paperback. US$5.99, Cdn$8.99.

Creating Love

Kay Kuzma. In what she has called her most important book, Kay Kuzma, of Family Matters Ministries, shares powerful stories and principles that can revolutionize your relationships and even turn obnoxious people into lovable ones.
0-8163-1382-2. Paperback. US$11.99, Cdn$17.99.

Order from your ABC by calling **1-800-765-6955,** or get online and shop our virtual store at **<www.adventistbookcenter.com>.**
•Read a chapter from your favorite book
•Order online
•Sign up for email notices on new products

Prices and availability subject to change.